Laurence W. M. (Laurence William Maxwell) Lockhart

Fair to see

Vol. II

Laurence W. M. (Laurence William Maxwell) Lockhart

Fair to see
Vol. II

ISBN/EAN: 9783337051624

Printed in Europe, USA, Canada, Australia, Japan

Cover: Foto ©ninafisch / pixelio.de

More available books at **www.hansebooks.com**

FAIR TO SEE

A NOVEL

BY

LAURENCE W. M. LOCKHART

AUTHOR OF 'DOUBLES AND QUITS'

IN THREE VOLUMES

VOL. II.

WILLIAM BLACKWOOD AND SONS
EDINBURGH AND LONDON
MDCCCLXXI

The Right of Translation is reserved

FAIR TO SEE.

CHAPTER XI.

The arrival of the day of "the gathering" brought a diversion, not unwelcome, perhaps, to any of the performers in this tragi-comedy.

It was to be a day full of events; for not only was there to be "a gathering" and a ball, but, as an interlude, suggested, no doubt, by the expected concourse of "the country-side," the candidate for the boroughs was in the evening to address the electors of the town of Ardmartin; so that the bill of fare held out inducements to all the world, and everybody said that all the world would be there. The weather was splendid, and so the party were conveyed to the scene of action—about fourteen miles distant—in an open break; Mrs

M'Killop having covenanted that a certain absence of state in the character of the vehicle should be balanced by its being drawn by four post-horses, which was very noble. One of the postilions, indeed, had a red jacket, while the other was in blue—an incongruity not perhaps altogether corrected by the very black eye which dimmed the lustre of the gentleman in red ; but this was a mere matter of detail : and what with Hamish on the box, his pipes adorned with a banner of the M'Killop arms quartered with those of M'Whannel, M'Cuaig, M'Kechnie, and a good many other rather guttural septs ; what with Mrs M'Killop inside, blazing like the fire of Baal, not to mention the chaster brightness of Eila and Morna,—it must be admitted that they made a brave appearance, on the whole. They were to dine and dress at the hotel, therefore there was luggage ; they were to luncheon *al fresco* at " the gathering," therefore there were hampers— bountiful, well-filled hampers—for the Cairnarvoch cook was a good cook, and the mistress of Cairnarvoch loved the handiwork of her handmaiden. Also there was wine ; for " there is to be no nonsense about the champagne,

M'Killop," had been much on Mrs M'Killop's lips for the two previous days; and there *was* no nonsense about it; so that the break, which was also to bring back Messrs Duncanson and Tainsh for their visit, if they preferred that to travelling separately, was by no means over-horsed with four.

Eila began the day very propitiously, in the brightest of moods. She was kindness itself to Bertrand; manœuvred him into a seat beside her in the break; told him it was a comfort in going to a stupid ball to feel that one was with a nice party, and therefore independent; hoped he and Captain Pigott would be very civil, and not desert them; wished to know *exactly* what he thought of her new hat, of which she herself was doubtful; and confided to him that she had selected and made up with her own hands a bouquet for his coat in the evening, which was "with her things" under charge of M'Kenzie, the spectral maid. A minute or two later, Bertrand was a little dashed by discovering that the same distinction was to be enjoyed by Pigott and her father; but rallied again on being assured that he should have first choice, as well as the advantage of her advice in his selection. And "I do hope you are not going in the Highland dress, Mr Cameron?" she added. It was desolation to Bertrand to confess that that garb and no other was in his portmanteau in the boot.

"I am sorry for that," said Eila; "because almost everybody else will wear it,—and the other is so much more distinguished on such an occasion; it looks, you know, as if you didn't care. I had quite made up my mind not to dance with any one in the Highland dress; but now, as, of course, I *must* dance with you, I shan't be able to make it a law for the evening, which would have been great fun, wouldn't it? It is very provoking. I do hope Captain Pigott is not to be in a kilt."

No; Bertrand was obliged to admit that his friend would certainly be in pantaloons.

"But I'll tell you what I'll do, Miss M'Killop. As soon as we get to Ardmartin I'll send a man back with a trap for my other things."

"Oh, please do—oh, thank you; yes, that will be such fun. Fancy sending nearly thirty miles! That *will* be delightful!"

"I would send round the world to—ahem!"

"Now I will tell you a secret," Eila interrupted, with great earnestness of eye;—"I am going to wear mauve!"

"Really!"

"Yes; and not a single bit of tartan. *That* ought to make them very angry!"

Who was to be made angry, and with what purpose, Bertrand did not pause to investigate, but assented unhesitatingly that it ought to rouse the most vindictive feelings.

"Mamma doesn't know."

"How lucky!"

"And not even Morna!"

"What a triumph of *finesse!*"

In such blissful converse, the fourteen miles were traversed all too rapidly; and they reached the ground where "the gathering" was to be held, in about two and a half minutes, as it appeared to Bertrand.

The term "gathering," in its technical sense of a coming together of various clans marshalled in warlike array by their chiefs, was not strictly applicable to the meeting at Ardmartin, as the clans did not parade in this formidable shape, but came, in independent units, to take part in the athletic games of the Gael, or to look on at them, or to see the "country-side" and the gala, and fulfil one of the chief ends of (Scottish) man in a patriotic consumption of the fluid staple of the district.

The ground where the meeting was to be held was both picturesque and well adapted to the purpose. It lay in a small circular valley, surrounded on all sides by hills that sloped gently down to a perfectly level centre, several hundred square yards in area. It was a natural amphitheatre, with a natural arena, affording the athletes ample space for all their cantrips, and to the spectators the best possible convenience for looking on. The country-people were already clustered in tier above tier on the hillside, the bright tartan which belonged to some part of the dress of the most of them, male and female, making the circle look like a gay fringe attached to the imperial robe of purple heather in which the hills were clothed. On one side, a certain space had been told off on the level, for the carriages of the gentry, and in the centre of this was a flag-staff, from which floated the golden banner of Scotland with its ruddy, ramping lion. In front of this position two kilted companies of Rifle

Volunteers were posted—as a guard of honour, it was alleged, but in whose honour, no one seemed quite to have ascertained. This mysterious force from time to time, apparently when it had nothing else to do, deployed into line on its leading company, opened ranks and vaguely presented arms, re-forming column again, and standing at ease, with a precision that must have satisfied any alarmist as to the safety of that part of her Majesty's dominions. It was attended by its band, consisting of a dozen rather swollen-looking Celts, who did not spare themselves—or the audience—but brayed with tremendous energy during the major part of the day; and altogether the Volunteers formed a conspicuous feature in the scene. Mr Tainsh was in command of them. Mr Tainsh was one of those men about whom all local offices of trust, emolument, and dignity seem to encrust themselves as by an inevitable law of nature; so, of course, he commanded the Riflemen; and if there had been a Volunteer flotilla in connection with Ardmartin, no one doubted that Mr Tainsh would also have been the admiral or commodore in charge of it. There was already a full muster of carriages of the county aristocracy—indeed there did not seem to be a niche for the Cairnarvoch party; and the postilions, demoralised by the haughty bearing of the family coachmen already on the ground, made no proper effort to assert themselves and squeeze into a place. Thus they were in difficulties, but help was at hand.

Pushing through the crowd, with a drawn sword in his hand, before which, and his local influence, all gave way, approached the deliverer. He looked very hot and flustered; and his uniform gave him rather the air of a fowl trussed for the table; but he was a pleasant sight to the people in the break, for he was the secretary of the games and managing steward of the meeting—in a word, Mr Tainsh.

He hailed the carriage from a distance with loud greetings, shook hands tumultuously with the whole party when he came up, said they were rather late, but he had postponed the commencement of the games, of course (with his eye on Eila), till their arrival, and had reserved for them the best place on the ground. Then he jumped on the back-step, and called out to the postilion with the black eye to put the spurs in and fear no evil. It was a great thing to be well with Tainsh on such a day as this. So they drove to their position, slowly past the line of carriages, Mrs M'Killop (whom, from her first arrival among them, the county had decided to ignore) doing her best, with a tremendous double eyeglass, to return the broadside of all the eyes in each, rearing her head up like some terrible sea-serpent about to spring, in a manner calculated to awe the boldest, and altogether running the gauntlet with much bravery and spirit.

" Dreadful-looking person ! "

" Quite an eyesore ! "

" Pretty girls, though."

" Oh no ; very bold and pert-looking."

" Who are these men ? "

" How can you ask ? "

" Nobody knows anything about such people."

" I am sure that red woman drinks."

" She is evidently very tipsy at this moment."

" How she stares ! "

" The termagant ! "

" The ogress ! "

One can imagine that the glances directed at the break by the utterers of such sentiments were not very amicable, and so estimate the weight of the guns Mrs M'Killop had to engage. Pigott was really delighted with the sensation they produced, and stared in a pleased wooden way (acting as a sort of auxiliary gunboat to his hostess) at the indignant *beau-monde.*

"Holloa! here's Bob West!" he cried out suddenly, as they approached, and for an instant halted beside a carriage of very distinguished appearance, outside of which was the gentleman in question.

"How are you, Bob?"

"By George! it's the Pig!" (by this swinish *sobriquet* our friend was known in pigeon-shooting circles). "You here! Wonderful! Where have you dropped from? Awfully glad to see you."

"I'll come back and talk to you presently."

"Do, my porker;" and they rolled on again.

"The Jook's carriage!" exclaimed Mrs M'Killop with bated breath (she had struck her topgallants, so to speak, on approaching the gracious vehicle). "Who is your very distinguished-looking friend, Captain Pigott?—a nobleman, of course?"

"Well, he's Bob West. No, he's not a nobleman; he is a lord, however, his papa being the very dilapidated Irish Marquess of something or other. He's a capital shot."

"A most refined-looking man. By the by, Captain Pigott, any friends you may wish to give luncheon to, will be welcome here, you know. Consider the break your own home, and use every freedom."

"You are very kind; I'll bring Lord Robert and present him. I am sure you will like him."

"He looks really fascinating; does he not, girls?"

The moment they got on to the ground, Bertrand felt a sort of chill presentiment that his good times were over for the day. His confidential intercourse with Eila abruptly terminated, and he saw her face change, and flush, and brighten with excitement, as she gazed on the concourse, recognising, no doubt, new worlds to conquer.

Instantly he was jealous, furiously jealous, of everything and everybody; of Tainsh when he came up like a conquering hero, swaying crowds and recalcitrant coachmen, with disgusting omnipotence; of a tall, dark, bearded man, on a private omnibus, with lavender gloves and a binocular, through which he appeared (the vampire!) to feast on Eila's beauty as long as they were in sight; of Bob West, who *was* a most insufferably pleasant-looking fellow, and had his eye on *her* at once; in short, of every male being within eyeshot of the break. When they were safely ensconced in a capital place at the head of the line, Tainsh said "he would now go and start them," inviting himself, with the easy grace of an emperor assured of his welcome, to return to luncheon, when, as he said to Eila, he would take *her* orders as to any change in the programme she might like to suggest (surely the "fellow" was "riding on the tip-top of his commission"), and also bring her the list of dances for the evening "as soon as it came down from the printer." Tainsh was, of course, managing steward of the ball, and had all the arrangement of it and everything else—being on this day an embodiment of pluralism and patronage; so that it was really a case of "Nisi Tainsh frustra." Eila perhaps fully realised this, for she was fascination itself to him, even going so far, apropos of some talk about bouquets, as to promise to confiscate, for the use of this "beast of a factor," the flowers destined for her papa, who, she said, would never miss them; whereupon Bertrand, unable to endure this levelling-up process, cried out, "Mr M'Killop can have my bouquet! It is heartily at his service!"

"But you haven't got one, Mr Cameron, have you?" retorted Eila. "I said I had some bouquets, and that *perhaps* I would give you one; but that was only if you behaved very well;" then, when Tainsh had gone away grinning, and she saw that Bertrand's face was furious and dark, she added, with her winsomest smile, "but as you always behave well, of course it will be yours, and" (*sotto voce*) "I flattered myself that you would not be so ready to part with a gift of *mine*."

Away clouds and tempests! away! avaunt! Retro Sathanas! "Part with it? I will wear it next my heart till I die." But, alas! this is only what Bertrand was *going* to cry out, when he was interrupted by a shrill exclamation from Eila, in chorus with several hundred female voices, and due to the letting-off of a field-piece, which had "played bang!" as

Hamish expressed it, in obedience to a signal from Tainsh when he left the carriage, and which meant that the games were to begin. Then in an instant all was stir and commotion, so that Bertrand could get no further hearing; and seeing the postilions moving off to stable their horses in the town, he got down hastily and ran after them, to arrange for the despatch of a messenger to Cairnarvoch for his things; finding, on his return, Eila and Morna established on the box-seat ("so cosily," the former said), *vice* Hamish, gone away to compete for something, so there was nothing for him but to get inside, and look gloomily on at the athletes.

The games were like all other games, which everybody has seen—for where are they not held, wherever a few Highlanders are gathered together, from Braemar to Borneo?

And a goodly sight they were, and pleasant it was to see the flower of the flower of the lusty and stalwart manhood of the world, taxing sinews of iron, and straining matchless powers of endurance, as the hammer was hurled, and the caber tossed, and the long stern race run up the rugged mountain-side, and the measure of a tall man's stature cleared with the lightness of the hunted deer,—and the wild grace, spirit, and enthusiasm of the glorious "strathspey;" while, at every feat or failure, a wave of deep sound, like the rolling boom of surf upon the shore, came from thousands of voices on the hill. Besides the more energetic exhibitions, the less violent part of the usual programme was duly fulfilled ; and the quoiters quoited, and the "best-dressed Highlanders at their own expense," paraded before often-puzzled judges ; and, above all things, the pipers piped in emulation, and everywhere over the hillside were little groups of umpires, and in the centre of each a competitor doing his best to enchant their ears—while, in every nook and dell, a performer not yet "called," tortured his yelling instrument up to the proper pitch of readiness, so that the air quivered with the sound of diffused piping, "giving a mere Englishman," as Pigott said, "the feeling of spending his day on board a steamer for ever in the act of making a temporary stoppage at a station.

The luncheon-hour came, and Pigott, who had gone to "look up" Bob West, brought back that noble Lord, who proved to be, exactly as Bertrand had feared, a most engaging fellow, blind to Mrs M'Killop's absurdities, observant of M'Killop, frank and jolly to Bertrand himself, and oh! so gay, so easy, so unembarrassedly *debonnair* and delightful to the young ladies, especially to *her* upon whom Bertrand felt that Bob West's noble eye rested with much too admiring an expression.

"Now you've come, my Lord," cried Mrs M'Killop, in delight, "we'll have luncheon. Pray step in, and come up to this end, where your Lordship will have a rest for 'his' back."

So his Lordship, who was not the least of a swell, but rather accused of being the companion of publicans and sinners, got in, somewhat crushed by the homage he received, and took up his position exactly under the heavenly elevation on which Bertrand's angel was perched. Dashed, moping, miserable, Bertrand himself allowed one person after another to pass above him, so that he finished in a seat at the door, whence he could command a fine view of Bob West handing up viands to the box-seat, always with some pleasantry which "took," or proffering goblets of champagne with remarks of an equivalent sparkle, and generally compassing the box-seat " with sweet observances."

And yet Bob West could eat at the same time very heartily, and drink really with spirit, and answer Mrs M'Killop's questions about the " Ditchess" whose guest he was, and assure Mr M'Killop that he was making a capital lunch, so cordially, that, if the thing had gone on long, M'Killop must inevitably have tackled him about " wool;" and altogether it was sackcloth and ashes for Bertrand; and when Bob, his luncheon finished, stood up, and was begged as a " favour" by the box-seat to smoke, and did so with his back to the company, and his face to *her* (who " blazed into him eighteen to the dozen," as Pigott subsequently reported), the cup quite ran over; and Bertrand began to think that a permanent residence on the tip-top of the Cordilleras was the DOOM to which he had better consign himself, with all convenient speed. He selected the Cordilleras as a nice desolate sort of mountains, where you can be cosily frozen to death, without any sort of fuss or trouble. The noble Lord seemed in no hurry to move; and when he had asked for a third tumbler of champagne, and lighted a fresh cigar, Mrs M'Killop, whose foible it was to sleep after meals, fearing to commit so grave a breach of etiquette in so aristocratic a presence, "thought she would take a turn," and impressed the wretched Bertrand into her service as escort, who went with her mechanically, and she ran him right under the guns again ; for, brave at all times, Mrs M'Killop was slightly pot-valiant now, and thirsted for the fray ; and so twice up and down the line of carriages she passed, tossing and fleering and glaring through her glass, and explaining to Bertrand, with very articulate enunciation, that there was no one here whom any one knew anything at all about, except the "Ditchess," with whom (*viâ* Bob West) she felt herself to be in a sort of *rapport*. From the line they passed to a judgment of "best-dressed Highlanders," and among the umpires whom should they find but Mr Duncanson ?

"You have never been near us, James !" exclaimed Mrs M'Killop, in a *quasi* hurt tone. "Very polite of you, I must say."

James explained, that having the entire cares of the meeting on his shoulders, it had been impossible for him to get away as he could have wished; but he hoped to visit the break before very long, and asked for Miss Morna.

"Oh, Morna is very well and very happy! I left her in charge of our friend, Lord Robert West—who is a monstrous agreeable young man—making them all die of laughing. You'd better go soon, or the luncheon will be all gone. His Lordship knows what's what, and has asked leave to bring some of his friends from 'the castle' to try the grouse-pie; go soon"—and Duncanson made short work of an old man, with a great deal of untanned hide about his body (and who announced that his model in dress was Gilian Glas of the seventh century or so), and went. And Mrs M'Killop, remembering an old dowager at the other end of the line who had looked spiteful, but whose eye she had failed to catch, took Bertrand up the line again, and having polished off the dowager by remarking under her very nose, after a careful inspection, "Just as I thought! Rouged, the teeth false, and the left eye artificial!" marched gaily back to her cantonments. Here things had by no means altered for the better. Bob West still occupied his old place; beside him, talking to Morna, was another man of the same type, with a splendid buccaneering auburn beard. On the step, in front of Eila, stood Tainsh rattling away, quite unabashed, and dividing Eila pretty fairly with his Lordship—just as the Lord Mayor of the day at a City banquet, can hold his own with all sorts of principalities and powers; while on the ground, waiting for *his* innings, but occasionally anticipating them by a bold swipe, stood that horrible, black-bearded, lavender-gloved vampire from the omnibus, who made up for his disadvantageous position by a far-carrying and rather plaintive play of eye. It was horrible. Duncanson was on the off step with a tumbler of champagne in one hand, trying to eye down the auburn buccaneer, in which he did not seem quite to succeed, perhaps because his mouth was so full of grouse-pie, a plate of which delicacy was before him on the foot-board.

The programme for the evening had just reached Tainsh "from the printer;" and as Bertrand came up, he heard a deal of petitioning for this dance and that, going on on the part of Bob West, Tainsh, and the murky villain down below.

"Really, Lord Robert," Eila was saying, "you are too avaricious! I have given you four already. No, no; I must be firm."

"Give me *all* the 'Hoolichans,' Miss Eila," cried Tainsh.

"Really, Mr Tainsh, you are too greedy" (*N.B.*—A noble Lord is "avaricious"—a factor, however prosperous, cannot rise above "greed"); "be contented with the first and the last: and then, you know, you have the country-dance, and you would insist on the 'Bonny Dundee' Quadrille."

"I only ask one favour, Miss M'Killop; I ask you to make me a sporting promise—don't read the composers' names, but promise me all the valses by Strauss in the programme. If they are many, I shall be in Paradise; if there are none, I shall go to bed—voilà." This (in a voice full of the grand colossal melancholy of a colossal Alpine horn wailing among the Alps) was the Vampire's contribution to Bertrand's misery. He grew sick at heart—he would stay there no longer—he would be off to the Cordilleras at once, and he started away from the carriage, in that sense.

"Mr Cameron!" He looked round; *she* was calling him. "You have not asked me for a dance; how unkind! and they are nearly all gone."

Every eye in and about the carriage was turned upon Bertrand, but his Highland blood was fairly up, and he confronted them all, even including *her*, with a fierce and haughty bearing; then said, in a cold, acrid (and as *he* imagined), thoroughly-indifferent-to-her voice, "Please don't keep one for me; I'm rather fastidious about floors; and I don't really think I should be quite equal to getting round on the kind of thing we are likely to have to-night. So sorry!" And, impervious to a mournful, pleading eye, and a sort of coaxing, deprecating pout of the lips, he turned and went. "I have made her *feel*," he said to himself, with savage exultation—"*feel!*" And so he had, no doubt, and all the others too; the feelings of the latter (not, it is to be hoped, of the former) were, however, mirthful and derisive.

"What's the matter with him?" laughed easy Lord Bob.

"Who *is* the beggar?" demanded the Buccaneer.

"I think I've seen him before," said the Vampire, still in his blow-bugle-blow tones; "or is it, tell me, is it only that he's so like Sidney Bancroft, in his most 'walking' and dignified moments?"

"He's making a precious fool of himself," cried Tainsh, who was perhaps a little jealous, and at all events could not have impertinences directed against the floor which he had "arranged" and "managed."

"As he always does," gobbled Duncanson.

No voice of defence came from the box-seat, although Morna's face flushed, and she looked as if she was going to speak almost; but from inside came a still, small, dry, rather languid voice.

"His name is Bertrand Cameron, if you want to know, and he's got more sense and 'go' in his little finger than all you fellows have in your united brains—except you, Mr Tainsh, and you, Mr Duncanson—because I don't know you well enough to take the freedom of speaking the truth yet. Poor Bertrand is awfully seedy. He had a touch of the sun on the hill the other day, and he hasn't been right since. I'll go and look after him. Don't finish all the champagne, Bob; you've been drinking like a camel for the last hour;" and Pigott followed his friend.

He did not find him, however, for he had turned abruptly off to the left and taken to the steep hillside at once. And up it he tore with the energy of a maniac, till he was spent and breathless, and perforce obliged to slacken his pace; after which, in a little, came cooler reflection, and then in a little came remorse, and then, in a little more, came repentance. After all, had he not "abdicated his functions?" (like the Peers when they don't happen to be in their normal condition of "exercising an intolerable oligarchical pressure.")

After all, was it her fault that she was so attractive that all the world came a-wooing? After all, had he not himself been a brute, a maniac, a ruffian? And oh! that look of tenderness, sorrow, simple, guileless WOE! How could he have turned from *that* with a flinty heart and flintier countenance? Hang the Cordilleras! he would go back to her; he would beg for forgiveness. And so, like the King of France, having marched up the hill, he marched down again; and there was Eila (having exchanged seats with Mrs M'Killop) sitting inside, all alone, looking desolate; and he went in beside her and made his peace; saying, in answer to her earnest and even suggestive inquiries, that he *had* been again "faint," and promptly receiving eau-de-Cologne from a glorified phial with a gold and turquoise top, taken from her own blessed pocket. And then he heard with rapture that, although her card was filled up, still for *him* she must try to make some arrangement — *Anglicé*, throw some one over; and learned, with a thrill, that she had *quite* decided (after mature thought) that his bouquet was to consist of a blush rose, supported by myrtle-leaves, jessamine, and heliotrope: and now was he happy? And he said he was happier than——, but he had no words to express what he meant; still he looked it pretty fairly, and they interogled strenuously in silence, for one brief ecstatic minute, when the accursed posters arrived to take them back to the town, the games being all over, "except the shouting," of which, by the by, they had soon more than enough; for presently arrived Hamish M'Erracher, furiously drunk and minus his bagpipes, which, having been overcome in a musical contest, he had (with the sensibility of a defeated Celt) obligingly thrown over a precipice. And Hamish swore, like any French soldier, that he had been betrayed and duped by one Parlane M'Farlane, beguiled by that "nestee, powterin' plŏckhēēd and răscāl" into inordinate whisky, so that the cunning of his hand and lip had failed him, and he was disgraced; but had a kick or so left in him yet, for he would fight then and there any man in honour of Mr M'Killop and the leddies — emphatically "annee man," not even excepting "fechting Geordie," who was understood to be the postilion whose honourable scars lent a sombre distinction to the M'Killop equipage.

Hamish gave much trouble, and frightened the ladies a good deal, but was eventually captured and led away by two constables, between whose grandmothers' maternal aunts and Mrs M'Killop he was heard to draw (in

Gaelic) comparisons altogether unfavourable to the former ladies. This trouble disposed of, they drove to the hotel for an early dinner, where all went merry as a marriage-bell—no Lord Bob, no Buccaneer, no Vampire to cast shadows over the banquet. It was all too short, however, to please Bertrand; for the ladies had to rest in the middle of a somewhat formidable day's work, and then they had to dress, which would be a work of time; so Mrs M'Killop withdrew the young ladies the moment dinner was over. When they were gone, M'Killop suggested that perhaps the two gentlemen might like to go to the meeting and hear the candidate for the boroughs explain his views to the electors of Ardmartin; he, M'Killop, not caring to go himself, thinking it unseemly, he said, as a mere sojourner in the district, to mix himself up with its politics.

"What do you say to going, Bertrand?" asked Pigott.

"Oh, I'll go with pleasure."

Bertrand was again in spirits, and would go anywhere or do anything; so off they went, leaving their host to devour the "Money Market and City Intelligence."

CHAPTER XII.

THE meeting was held in a chapel of one of those mysterious and numerous dissenting sects, the shepherds of which appear now to exercise in Scotland, that supreme political influence formerly enjoyed in Ireland by the Roman Catholic priests; and, in this building, a large and noisy assembly was already congregated, when our friends entered. Much whisky had been imbibed on the ground during the day, and more still in the town, by earnest topers, who, regarding time occupied in visiting the games as the merest misuse of golden moments diverted from the real business of the occasion, had stayed at home and toped earnestly. At the games the whisky had "lain" very fairly during the day, Hamish's escapade being almost the only call upon the services of the force; but, towards evening, as the carriages rolled into the town after the games were over, their drivers had to contend with a good deal of staggering latitudinarianism, which required the road, and the whole road, not to mention an occasional bold slice out of an adjacent field or two, to make anything like a satisfactory course to Ardmartin. And now the saturnalia had begun in earnest, and as Pigott and Bertrand passed down the street they found themselves in the midst of it, as it raved, and screeched, and quarrelled, and danced, and hugged, and wept, and sang, and fought through the town, or reposed in sodden content in the gutters, or philosophised in muttered broken apostrophes to lamp-posts, pumps, and such other objects as, from the nature of things, can be button-holed to a certainty. Inside the meeting itself there was to be found pretty nearly every stage of intoxication — the furious, the imbecile, the philosophic, the declamatory, the maudlin. The air was loaded with alcoholic fumes; a cubic foot of it resolved into its chemical elements might have produced a bottle or so of fair Glenlivet.

Yells of impatience, political cries, local

witticisms, personal altercations, made a babel of strange sounds. There was a party for smoking, and a party opposed to it — as sacrilegious; so that pipes were lighted and smashed, from a theological point of view. Then bottles were handed about, sucked at, fought for, dropped, broken. Songs were called for, toasts proposed, hissed, cheered, and hooted. Never was such a wild, orgiastic hurly-burly in any place of worship, save perhaps that of Bacchus.

This was a specimen section of the stratum in which Mr Disraeli expected to find calm, temperate, patriotic Conservatism, when he leaped, with nine-tenths of his party, down the coal-pit to look for it.

Presently there was a lull as a procession entered by a side-door from the vestry, and ascended to the platform, which was arranged round the desk from which the "leader of song" on Sabbaths conducted the praises of the congregation. The procession was really sober. It was headed (of course) by Mr Tainsh, who "conducted" the candidate, and was composed of the respectables of the town, with here and there a Liberal laird (or rather

" bonnet-laird "), looking as if on that occasion at least he rather regretted his political creed.

A certain Bailie M'Candlish came to the front of the rostrum and was saluted with various cries.

"See till Caundlish!" "A sang frae Caundlish!" "Pit on yer specs, man." "Stick in, Bylie!" "Wha boucht the deed coo?" The last—an allusion apparently to some questionable transaction of the Bailie's which divided the sentiment of the place—produced a terrific uproar, in a slight lull of which he, however, contrived to move that his honourable friend Mr Tainsh (of course) should take the chair; and a storm of indiscriminate howling being assumed as assent, Mr Tainsh marched into the precentor's box, bowed to Pandemonium, said (amid interruptions) that they knew the object of the meeting (which could only have been true in a very restricted sense), and that, without farther parley, he begged to introduce Mr Platt-Crump from London, who was recommended to the attention of the boroughs by that eminent friend and adviser of the "working man," Mr John Bright.

Under the ægis of this great name Mr Platt-

Crump, on coming forward, was received with immense applause. He was a tall, thin, wiry, middle-aged man, with rather a hungry face, understood to be a barrister, and justifying the belief by a certain cosy, confidential, and withal fluent method of speaking, as well as by a forensic habit of tucking his thumbs into the arm-holes of his waistcoat. The people shouted "Bravo!" and "Go it!" and thus encouraged, Mr Platt-Crump went it, and no mistake. He began by saying that he was, before everything else, "progressive,"—which might have been true once, but, by his own subsequent showing, was at present rather incredible, Mr Crump having apparently got as far as was possible, until some one was kind enough to invent a bran-new set of institutions for Mr Crump to "progress" through and demolish with his inexorable hoofs. He then proceeded to show that he was not merely a reforming broom, but also a political petard; and if only the good folks of Ardmartin would be kind enough to place him in position, and apply the match, he was prepared to blow everything, with one or two very trifling exceptions, to smithereens.

If he was asked, "Would he support a measure for the abolition of the law of hypothec?" Mr Platt-Crump's reply was that he would strain every sinew and muscle to get it passed.

Of the Game Laws? all his energy should be devoted to digging up that subtle r-r-root of an effete feudalism.

Of the restrictions upon Trades-unions? he would say, "Erase from the statute-book such a discreditable BLOT."

Of the State Church? he would cry, "Down with it!"

Of the Commander-in-Chief? he would sign the death-warrant of that entirely bloated official.

Of Bishops in the House of Lords? he would sweep these sanctimonious dotards from their pride of place.

Of the House of Peers itself? that was a delicate question, but Mr Platt-Crump was prepared to face it with calm, and he would tell the Peers (frankly) that vitality having passed from them, they were now a mere "excrescence" for which he knew of only one remedy, and that was "the knife, gentlemen—

the incisive, trenchant knife of radical reform."
(Cheers.) As to University Tests—but they
were too nauseous a subject, and Mr Platt-
Crump turned his head aside and archly
feigned a temporary sickness, thereby delicately suggesting the fate that awaited *them*.
Then the army in its present state must be
abolished, and some popular substitute provided—(officered, if possible, by working men);
in its present state it was intolerable. Would
any one kindly tell him why the sweat of toil-
ing, moiling millions should be squandered
upon a *sham*, a *farce*, that gilded lordlings
(ever ready to batten upon the inwards of the
working man) might r-r-ruffle it in the haunts
of aristocratic sensuality? (Immense applause,
but apparently a good deal of irritation about
the chairman's scalp.) Yes, he would abolish
that and everything else — everything, that
was to say, that weighed upon the working
man, was distasteful to his feelings or repug-
nant to his conscience. He would abolish
every tax that was any sort of restriction upon
the enjoyments to which the working man felt
he had not merely a bias but a claim. The
deficit thence resulting he would meet by

dealing with the land in a bold spirit. (Loud cheers.)

If he (Platt-Crump) swayed the destinies of this great country, every working man should begin his day, to use the impressive, he might say epigrammatic, words of his illustrious friend John Bright—(thunders of applause)—at a "free breakfast-table;" and—though in this, perhaps, he advanced boldly—starting from the dictum of that great man, he would extend that freedom to every meal of which honest labour partook in the course of the day, even topping up at night with a free pipe of tobacco and a free glass of toddy. (Frantic applause and much laughter.)

Then, of course, came Mr Platt-Crump's peroration that there was only one MAN who could secure these inestimable advantages for the working classes, and he would do it—ay, he *would* do it, sure as his name was a name before which bigots and oligarchs quailed, and tricksy reactionaries trembled in their spangles and their motley—(sensation, and a voice, "Jimsie, gie's the dottle o' yer pipe!")—sure as his name was WILLIAM EWART GLADSTONE, the only great statesman with a brain (John

Bright excepted), the only great statesman with a conscience, the only great statesman with a heart, all, with every other item of his system, mental and corporeal, entirely devoted to the people from whom he sprang.

Have faith in Gladstone. Give him a following, and he will do it. Then came the obvious deduction, " Therefore rally round Platt-Crump and support first-rate talent." And Mr Platt-Crump sat down smiling among the ruins, as it were, of everything except Mr Gladstone and the working man, amid hurricanes of applause. There was hardly an adverse sentiment expressed even by the soberest of the audience. A very mealy baker, indeed, loudly stated his opinion that Mr Platt-Crump was "naething but a bletherin' speldran;" a view supported with a good many quaint oaths by a mason, perhaps from some hazy professional feeling, that though a first-rate puller-down of edifices, Mr Crump had contrived to hide his light as a constructor under a very comprehensive bushel. These reactionaries having being eliminated after a tough resistance, Mr Crump was subjected to the process of "heckling"—that is, cross-examination by the more representative men of the meeting ; and here his success was not so marked. It was all very fine and very easy to deal in a set speech with large imperial questions, particularly when he had nothing to suggest but a saw-and-pick-axe policy ; but every locality has its own pet political maggot, and with a Scotch constituency there are two subjects at all times tender, sacred, and ticklish—the Sabbath and liquor (the irreverence of the collocation is not with the writer, but in the deplorable fact). Mr Crump had either been badly posted up on these questions, or he had got muddled by the row and the alcoholic atmosphere ; for upon being asked by a hoary old man with a reverend quaver in his voice, what his views were as to trading on "the Saw-ă-ă-bath" (here the quaver came out strongly), he began to bounce away about the working man being clearly entitled to buy his bit of bacon or his bit of baccy on any day in the week, and (jocularly) the better day the better deed. Similarly, as to Sunday places of recreation, Mr Platt-Crump thought that the working man, who had been moiling all the week, was not to be denied such amusement as might be in harmony with his own conscience. He was for perfect freedom. No one would deprecate more strongly than he any attempt to coerce the working man into an unwilling visit to a tea-garden of a Sunday; but, at the same time, he would equally deprecate any attempt to shut the tea-garden against the working man, if it was on that day his pleasure to visit that tea-garden. Murmurs had symphonied the whole course of this explanation, but at its conclusion they came to a head; the iteration of the word tea-garden was out of harmony with the spirit of the meeting, and a storm of disapprobation burst upon the bewildered Crump. "Remember the Saw-ă-ă-bath-day, to keep—" began the ancient querist; but his voice was drowned by the tumult, from which an occasional shrill cry shot out distinctly, such as "Awtheist!" "Blăsphaymer!" "Polly, pit the kettle on!" "Doon wi' the Pope!" "Bash him on the heed, Tainsh!" "Stap him up the chumley, Bylie!" and so on. Mr Tainsh having with difficulty procured silence, and rapidly consulted with Mr Platt-Crump, stated that the candidate would make an explanation, which after a time he was allowed to do; and which was to the effect that what he had said was merely a casual, ill-considered *résumé* of the general feeling of the Liberal party, including Mr Bright—(cries of "No, no; it's a big lee!" &c. &c.)—on the question. For himself, he had no strong bias either way; and if he became their Member, would consult their views and vote as they, in their wisdom, might direct. This appeased the assembly pretty well, except the reverend quaverer, who left the room expressing his conviction that Mr Platt-Crump was a "Laa-o-di-cayan," in addition to being a "foolish Galatian" and "a tinkling cymbal."

Then a determined-looking, stout, red-faced man rose and said that a question of grave interest to all thinking men, was involved in the proposal to enact a Permissive Liquor Law. He (the red-faced man) hoped Mr Platt-Crump was prepared to grapple with that question in a bold, decided, and thoroughly British spirit.

Here poor Crump was in terrible difficulties. The constituent group consisted of some five or six boroughs. These all agreed in the grand testing shibboleth "Gladstone," and the worship of one or two similar fetishes were matters of course; but in other respects they often differed. An opinion that was dogmatic in one, was indifferent in another, and on some questions there was open antagonism between them.

Thus in A the cry might be, "Down with the Church!"
" B " " "Death to the Rabbit!"
" C " " "A man may marry his grandmother!"
" D " " "Hypothec no more!"
" E " " "Man was made for the Sabbath!"

But A would raze the Church, and yet not marry his grandmother; while B, if you would only exterminate the rabbit, was prepared to let both the Church and his grandmother alone; and so on with infinite permutations and combinations, difficult for a poor man to carry always in his head who was speechifying, and being "heckled" day after day, and night after night, till he hardly knew which was uppermost—his head or his feet.

Thus Crump had forgotten all about the specialty of the town of Ardmartin; and so he, in his difficulty, thus reasoned with himself: "To abolish is liberal, to oppose is conservative; but you can't abolish what doesn't exist—whereas, if you oppose a new idea, however fallacious, you are in danger of condemnation as a Tory;" and therefore, after vainly trying to discern by the sodden faces of the audience what would be popular, he stammered out that it was "a large question—a *very* large question," he might go the length of saying "an *excessively* large question," "*and a broad question*" into the bargain. It was a question, he was free to confess, which had puzzled his head, ay, and wiser heads than his —being, in fact, one of those complicated problems which abound in a state of society resulting from an old civilisation, and a highly artificial condition of things in general.

But here the red-faced man jumped up and said that he was a plain man (which was incontrovertible), and that he had no relish for "hocus-pocus." "Would Mr Platt-Crump kindly abstain from hocus-pocussing him, and say 'yes or no'? Would he or would he not support a Permissive Liquor Bill?"

Thus spurred to the edge of the precipice, Mr Platt-Crump jumped over it and said he would support such a bill.

There was a solemn portentous silence for a few moments, and then came the ringing voice of the red-faced man with these words: "In that case, sir, I shall not support *you*; and I think I can pledge myself that nine-tenths of the gentlemen here present will follow my example."

Now the murder was out; the querist was the leading distiller of a district abounding in distilleries; half the people in the room were somehow or other connected with his trade, and the entire assembly tenderly sympathised with it as consumers.

"I hate humbug and cant, sir," added the red-faced man; "and I move that this meeting has no confidence in your political views; also, that they are entirely unworthy of a great nation."

A hundred seconders rose to their feet, and Tainsh was called upon to put the motion to the meeting. He declined upon some technical ground; and immediately, with the yells of Pandemonium, a rush was made to the platform, and the last things Bertrand and Pigott saw, as they left the place, were Platt-Crump vindicating his character as a progressive by a rapid flank movement towards the vestry, heavily salivated by a mob of pursuers, and Tainsh besieged in the pulpit, dodging missiles with surprising activity, and holding the position with the desperate valour of a Maori chief, alone, surrounded in his "pah," but resolved not to be taken alive.

Yet, as a matter of fact, Crump was eventually elected. He had been more successful in hocus-pocussing the other boroughs, probably, so that no opposition had been started; and now it was too late for the good folks of Ardmartin to organise one. So Crump went to Parliament, and is perhaps, at this hour, a tractable member of that wondrous majority; and if so, no doubt one of those poor devils—those dumb, delegate dogs who are bullied all round—who tremble at the bleating of the constituent flock, and crouch before the awful eye of the remedial but acid shepherd-in-chief.

"What do you think of that?" laughed Bertrand, when they were clear of the meeting.

"Think of it, my good fellow? Please don't let us think of it—it really makes me feel more inclined to cry than to laugh. We used to be able to look down upon—laugh at, if you please—the political life and customs of most other countries; but is there in all Europe, or perhaps even in America, to be seen any political exhibition so low, so filthy, so degraded as this we have just left? You blessed Scotchmen shake your solemn heads over the Irish difficulty, but, by George! you're as bad for old England as the Irish are, or worse; and what with Scotch Radicalism and Irish Fenianism and Ribbonism, England is between Scylla and Charybdis—destined, I fear, to sink. Platt-Crump ought to be boiled in some of that red-faced ruffian's whisky. Apropos, do you know if they give any decent sort of suppers at these gathering balls?"

"Oh, I suppose so."

"I hope they do; it was a wretched dinner, and I'm hungry already. Well, here's the hostel, and I suppose it is time to adorn."

CHAPTER XIII.

When Bertrand Cameron reached his room in the hotel after his return from the political meeting, he found to his joy, that the black garments which were to enable him to look "as if he didn't care" at the ball, had arrived from Cairnarvoch.

And oh! on the dressing-table there was *the* bouquet—there was the blush rose with its promised supporters; and—what was this? Could he believe his eyes? a pencilled memorandum! with these ravishing words—" The rose was a little shaky, so I have wired it; and the bouquet is fastened with *my own hair*—are you pleased?—E. M."

Too much happiness! to wear a rose, her gift, was sufficiently intoxicating; but there was a maddening, delirious joy in wearing a rose that she had actually wired! Happy, hallowed, sacred flower!

But great though the honour (and the bliss) of wearing a bouquet fastened by her hair, her hair could not be allowed to perform any such menial function. No, no: its place was obviously next his heart: and so he began to unwind the single silky thread that bound the flowers together, softly singing the while, from "Fair Helen of Kirkconnel," the appropriate verse—

> "Oh, Helen [Eila], fair beyond compare!
> I'll mak' a garland of thy hair,
> Will bind my heart for evermair
>   Until the day I dee."

Then, having unwound it, he tried to fondle the thread, dropping it often in that rather difficult process, and being compelled to search for it with a candle over a floor which had by no means been swept diligently; so that by the time it was finally captured and placed in an envelope for enshrining purposes, and by the time he had sufficiently venerated the bouquet, and mumbled the memorandum (which was eventually consigned to his purse in a somewhat soppy condition), a good half-hour had elapsed, and he was obliged to make a desperate scramble of his toilette, and descended very doubtful if his *tenue* quite came up to the devil-may-care standard it was expected to attain.

He found the party all assembled in the room where they had dined. *She*, as predicted, was in mauve, and without a scrap of tartan—almost without ornament, indeed; some white clustering flower in her hair, and bouquets of the same on the skirt of her dress, being excepted. Nothing could be purer, more ungarish, more faultless in the style of severe simplicity.

Morna was looking very pretty; she was in white, but she had not escaped her mother's tartanising touch—being to a certain extent "trimmed" with the national material. Still, she could bear it well, and, with her type of looks and complexion, might have sat for the portrait of an ideal "Bonnie Lassie of Scotland."

But what pen could describe, or what pencil limn, or what brush do justice to, the terrible grandeur of Mrs M'Killop? She was one of those spectacles—like Vesuvius in full eruption, or the Jung Frau in a thunderstorm—before which the bravest hold their breath for a time.

The folds of her dress were billowy and

oceanic; white ostrich-plumes surged round her head; gems of Ocean and of Ind flashed all over her body. Then, as for tartan, she had fully recognised the claims of half-a-dozen clans to be represented in her attire. Her person was told off into cantons, as it were, each sacred to a clan, and garnished with its colours. Thus, for example, her heart—the metropolitan canton, so to speak—was covered with a streaming cockade of the M'Whannel tartan, the colours of which not inaptly symbolised the thunder-and-lightning qualities attributed by their descendant to that extinct volcano; the right shoulder was occupied in force by the M'Cuaigs; the M'Kechnies skirmished promiscuously over her skirts,—and so on. Nothing but the roar and crash of artillery could have adequately heralded the entry of such a being into any assembly.

The ball was to be held in a room attached to the hotel. The hour had arrived, the scraping of violins was audible, the party were impatient to be gone, but Mrs M'Killop would not hear of it as yet. "If we sneaked in early," she explained, "it would look as if we were ashamed of ourselves: we must wait till the

Ditchess has gone in, and then no one can make any remark."

Nothing could be more intrepid. The Duchess was graciously pleased to be rather early; and before long, a scout detached for intelligencing purposes having brought back word that " her Gress and a' the muckle folk frae the Castle " were at that moment entering the ball-room, Mrs M'Killop figuratively drew her sword, called her troops to "attention," and marched them off to the scene of action. In the order of march, she led, supported by Pigott; Eila followed with Bertrand ; while M'Killop, much out of his element, brought up the rear with Morna.

The Duchess had seated herself at the right side of the room, and at the end farthest from the door ; around her were " a' the muckle folk frae the Castle ; " below them again, each party took up its position on entering, no one having had the courage to occupy the post *vis-à-vis* to the Duchess, which, as well as the upper half of the seats on the same side, was empty.

Rearing her head and tossing it, so that the ostrich-plumes acted as a sort of " punkah " to the bystanders, Mrs M'Killop led her party straight up the centre of the hall, stately and slow, and occupied the vacant place of distinction right opposite the Castle party. Much sensation was produced; every eye in the room was fixed on the little detachment and its audacious leader. There was a sudden audible buzz, composed of low laughter, stifled giggling, murmured exclamations of surprise, disapprobation, admiration, eager query, and rapid response. Mrs M'Killop said to herself, " Ha ! ha ! " like the war-horse; and, promptly unlimbering, opened fire at the opposing line through her great gold eye-glasses, with a vigour and concentration on individual points that overbore resistance. One of the most impertinent youngsters in the Foreign Office, who thought to cope with her, and stared at her " in the whites of the eyes " for half a minute, discoursing the while with a playful smile on his face, and his head perked critically awry, to a young lady who was " laughing quite furiously, you know, at the dreadful creature," fairly quailed and cowered before her scathing glance, suddenly smoothing his features into respectful solemnity, and muttering, " Don't laugh, please

—don't laugh; don't even look, or she'll come over and stwike us."

And so *he* was done for; and, in rapid succession, Mrs M'Killop mowed down scores of other foes—male and female—sparing neither age nor sex, except only the "Ditchess," partly because she *was* a duchess, and partly as being the friend of Bob West. Many of the men, however, paid little attention to the great woman, for the two lovely girls by her side were without anything approaching to a rival in the room; and many a yearning glance was cast across to those sweet heather-bells blooming so exquisitely, albeit in the shadow of that volcanic mountain of a mamma. Not a few wished they had the courage to seek for an introduction; but how cross the neutral ground raked by the fire of their own division, not to speak of the lava pouring from Mrs M'Killop's optics?—and not a few registered a vow that, when the evening had sufficiently advanced, the supping set in, and the dancing become vigorous, this object should be achieved. But the Cairnarvoch party had not been in this rather embarrassing position for many minutes, when Mr Tainsh rapidly entered the room. Apparently he had escaped uninjured from the "pah," and was again in uniform, wearing on his right breast a tricolor badge of universal management and stewardship, and, pinned ostentatiously over his (abominable) heart, *the* bouquet—*her* bouquet. Up the hall came the factor, easy, confident, and smirking, received with words and looks of goodwill by all and sundry as he passed.

He reached the Duchess; he approached her as if she had been a mere woman; spoke, even laughed, confidentially with her; then bowing, turned, went into the middle of the room, and clapped his hands. Whereupon, just as if Mr Tainsh had been a caliph or a grand vizier in the Arabian Nights, strains of exquisite music burst forth, and the ball began. Bertrand turned swiftly to Eila with a look of entreaty in his eyes; but her eyes saw him not, or "seeing would not see," for they were pervading the room, flashing from one group to another, with lightning rapidity. Whom was she looking for? It is needless, however, to follow her eyes, or the investigation, for almost instantly an opaque body was in front of her, ambling and bowing, and neither to be looked over nor looked through—Mr Tainsh.

"Our dance, I think, Miss Eila," exclaimed the factor, hooking out an arm that would not be gainsaid. Eila chased a cloud no bigger than a man's finger-nail from her face, and cordially assented; but had Mr Tainsh a *vis-à-vis*? Yes, Mr Tainsh had arranged all that; no less a person than the Earl of Hummums was to face them, along with Miss M'Corkindale of Collieshangie, the well-known heiress. And where were they to dance? right up at the top of the room, among all the grandees! Tainsh was really a jewel! And they did dance there; and Tainsh, riding on the top of his success—for he had managed everything for everybody—made everything pleasant for everybody, and was therefore (for the day) popular with everybody — was no laggard in his wooing, but went in to win, and made the running at such a terrific pace that Eila felt thankful when the quadrille was over, Mr Tainsh having traversed, in ten minutes, ground only to be got over in as many weeks by ordinary mortals, and having left almost nothing to be said but the burning words of a proposal in due form—which was not Eila's way of doing business, by any manner of means. The next dance struck up; it was a valse; it was a Strauss; and there was the Strauss-adoring Vampire right opposite, lounging beside the Duchess, apparently as blind to the existence of Eila, as he was deaf to the strains of the master he adored. It was puzzling; would he waken up and come? No; he was sitting down—the wretch!

Eila would *show* him. Bertrand found Eila in this frame of mind, offered himself with eyes full of meek love, was accepted, and away they went.

Gliding, drifting, dreaming, floating away upon waves of that narcotic melody—so full of love-pathos, so full of the harmonious whispers that befooled poor Faust—the very singing voice of sin and folly, if you will—but oh, so delightful! oh, so deplorably delightful to poor fools and sinners — the many that we are!

Bertrand, with his German education, his athletic form, and his faultless ear, was an ideal partner; Eila was, it is needless to say, also an ideal partner; and therefore, ye who have loved and valsed to perfection, and have combined the two movements, can imagine the state of drivelling beatitude in which the conclusion of the dance—the first valse with the beloved one—left our poor friend. Tainsh, even without the assistance of all his men, might probably have raised "Humpty-Dumpty," but *he* couldn't take his partner up into the seventh heaven; no, the factor, facting never so wisely, could not do *that*.

Bertrand looked into Eila's eyes where the light of dreamland still lingered, and felt that at that moment it was twenty to one against Mr Tainsh or any other factor, or any other man. Alas! it was but for a moment. The dance was over, and there was Bob West expecting his innings; so that, perforce, Eila dropped instantly from the seventh heaven—and, in truth, seemed to console herself very speedily with the noble earth-worm who was waiting to receive her, "rather fearing there *might* be a difficulty about another dance for Bertrand, but she would see later on."

Meantime Duncanson, looking in his Highland dress really a fine personable ghillie, had danced twice with Morna, and was rather clamorous in a dispute with the Buccaneer (who had arrived late, having, *very* apparently, dined), about the third dance, which each claimed; and one being a snob and the other a gentleman (who had dined), the discussion was rather loud and unpleasant to the fair apple of discord; and she said, with considerable spirit and acumen, "I think there is only one way of arranging it; I won't dance with either of you."

Bertrand, hearing this verdict, straightway offered himself, was accepted, went away with her, followed by four flaming eyes, and was as lugubrious a partner as could have been found within the four seas. And so the ball went on. Eila "Hoolican'd" with Mr Tainsh, and "Bonny-Dundee'd" with Mr Tainsh, valsed with Bob West, quadrilled with the Buccaneer, valsed with Bob West again, and then with two very pleasing friends of his; and whenever Bertrand ventured to offer himself, with love-sick eyes, he always found that there was a difficulty which at some remote future period *might* be got over. So *he* determined to *show* Eila; and went away, resolving to devote himself to Morna, over whom an intermittent fight seemed to smoulder on the part of the Buccaneer and Mr Duncanson during the entire evening; but found that there are two to a bargain, Morna saying coldly that, having already given him one dance, and having already made more engagements than she usually cared to make, she must decline his further partnership; and when he had begged and prayed in vain, he went away in a foaming rage with the whole Cairnarvoch party.

In this condition of mind, he was hailed by a splendid county magnate who had identified him as the heir of Aberlorna, and who fussed over him, and was quite a father to him, and must introduce him to his family (a hungry-looking wife and five *very* hungry-looking daughters), and to all the rest of the county—and did so; and to the Duchess, by whom, as by them all, he was most graciously received. And so he began to dance, literally, a series of war-dances (at Eila), taking first one daughter of the Duchess, and then another, up to the seventh heaven, similarly accommodating the heiress of Collieshangie, and many other young ladies, and never casting so much as a glance at the cruel fair who saw all his doings (though she never looked at *him*), and yet persevered in a mad career of Bob West, his pleasing friends, Mr Tainsh, and, at last, the Vampire, whose recollections of Strauss and Eila were miraculously revived after supper, and whose plaintive eye rested on her permanently thereafter with a look of champagny pathos.

Meantime Mrs M'Killop, not a foe being left unvanquished, had decided to shift her headquarters to the card-room (Tainsh had arranged for a card-room), and Pigott (not a dancing man, and all his female friends being occupied in the dance) had taken her there at her suggestion. There they had found, prowling forlorn, two elderly gentlemen wearing the air of Clubs rather than of Courts, and a rubber was immediately instituted, followed by another and another and another, with pauses for refreshment, Mrs M'Killop visiting the supper-room twice with Pigott, and once with each of the clubby men, not to mention several raids in the same direction under Mr Tainsh, who was everywhere, and all things to everybody.

So Mrs M'Killop ate and drank and rose up

to play, and *vice versâ*, and was merry, and made money, and had a row with one of the clubby old men about a revoke which she alleged he had made, but which he indignantly repudiated, asking, with outspread palms and high shoulders, "if it was likely (as a mere matter of common-sense) that a man who played daily and nightly at 'The Arlington' should revoke?" to which Mrs M'Killop replied, that "it was indifferent to her whether he played at Arlington, at Darlington, at Cairo, Copenhagen, or Kirkintilloch, but he *had* revoked;" whereupon the clubby man caved in, and altogether Mrs M'Killop thoroughly enjoyed herself. So much so, indeed, that the small hours passed on, and the bigwigs went away, taking Lord Bob, the Vampire, and all Eila's admirers with them; and still Mrs M'Killop sat on, forgetful of her charge. In this way Eila was left desolate, under care of her papa, who (after having been mistaken seven times for a waiter, and addressed once in that capacity, as a "gay old crocodile" by a comic youngster) had lurked about in all sorts of mysterious corners during the evening, and only emerged with the departure of the grandees; but the band still played ravishingly, and there was Bertrand careering with Miss M'Corkindale (who was to sleep in the hotel), and there was the Buccaneer (who, being a buccaneer, had no notion where he was to sleep, and didn't care) careering with Morna, and Mr Tainsh was away seeing the swells off the premises, and she, the Queen of the Evening, had no one left to do her reverence. It was dreadful; she looked pale, dejected. Bertrand saw it. For a second time that day, remorse, pity, wild love, seized upon his heart, so that he recklessly abandoned the heiress of Collieshangie to her mamma, and flew to his angel.

"At last, Mr Cameron!" said the angel, "when there is positively no one left to dance with but that hideous person you have just left; at last!"

"But, Miss M'Killop, I asked you six times, and you were always better engaged."

"*Better* engaged! oh, Mr Cameron!—when you knew, too, that I was only trying to clear off my engagements with all these tiresome men, that we might have some nice, long dances together, one after another! after *all* your promises! I shall *never* believe in you again."

" But I didn't know."

"*Oh*, Mr Cameron!"

" But how *could* I know ?"

"Oh, Mr Cameron!"

" But tell me."

"Some people can understand without words, what they are to do, and to expect; others require to have everything spelt out to them. Now I am going to say no more about it. I do hope we are going immediately."

" Oh, but forgive me—forgive me, or I shall be—so—wretched."

" How tragical you are! Very well, I forgive you."

She held out her hand playfully; he took it; he squeezed it—he positively did; and it was not withdrawn.

" I am dreadfully tired; please take me to the supper-room—I have never been there yet —and give me some champagne," said the angel, after her hand had been at length relinquished.

Bertrand took her away. A mist cleared from his mind; he had been under a misapprehension; to his gross, crass intellect some gracious implication of a promise had been impalpable; he was a dolt, a brute,—almost an assassin. But he atoned for it now, as they sat in the supper-room together; and he breathed forth his passionate penitence, and made all sorts of wild spasmodic approaches to the subject which was maddening his brain, though he never quite got up to the breach; and gave her up his bouquet, which she remarked to be faded, and took from him and affected to throw away, but didn't—he saw *that*—giving him instead (at his suggestion) one of the white bouquets from her dress, which he kissed *before her very eyes* and plunged inside his waistcoat, intimating that, on his death, it would be found there, and might be reclaimed by the owner; and, in fact, "went it" at a perfectly killing pace, and still read in her eyes "En avant!" and "Excelsior!"

But his hour was not as yet; for, just as things were boiling up very satisfactorily to a climax, in came Mrs M'Killop with much simulated wrath, and cleared them off. The break was at the door, she said, and they had been looking for Eila "all over the village for hours—*hours.*" So there was nothing for it but to go; and, after a tender muffling scene, they went; and the break, after some little waiting for Mr Duncanson (whose difficulty with the Buccaneer had culminated in the cloak-room, and resulted in the latter gentleman fastening on Mr D.'s nose with a desperate tenacity, from which he was with the greatest difficulty detached by Mr Tainsh), drove away, as the sun was rising above the hills, showing the party to be a little pale and worn, but touching Bertrand's prophetic and poetic soul with a sense of analogy and fitness and peace.

CHAPTER XIV.

THE campaign which Mr Tainsh had opened with so much vigour at the ball, was prosecuted during the next succeeding days at Cairnarvoch, in the same spirit; yet, at the close of each day, Mr Tainsh was surprised and mortified to find that, in point of fact, he had made no progress; he was still only on the brink,— the very position he had reached at the ball in the first quadrille with Eila. Morning after morning he registered a vow that that day's sun should not set upon his suspense; but night found him still baffled, still *in statu quo*. Yet he said to himself that it was not his fault—and indeed he said truly; for he was troubled with none of the sensitive, shrinking, self-depreciating tremors which afflict lovers of a more refined fibre; he had pretty nearly convinced himself that he was acceptable, and would be accepted, and that all he had to do was to bring the matter forward in a formal shape. There was a slight difficulty about that, of course, but it was a mechanical difficulty. At the worst, it was a question of æsthetics as to time, place, and circumstances, as to the phrases to be adopted, the gesture employed, and so forth. As a man not versed in such matters—as a man who had not considered love before, except as a matter affecting a client, and likely to result in the drawing of a marriage-contract for "the parties"—it was not wonderful, perhaps, that Mr Tainsh should be thus sanguine; for of a surety Eila was everything that was delightful and propitious, blessed him with her brightest glances, distinguished him in many ways with her favour, only now and then giving a whet to his appetite, which might have been blunted with too much saccharine matter, in the shape of a word or a look to Bertrand, which brought the factor up to an exaggerated state of keenness in a moment—for, of course, he was jealous of Bertrand; with all his assurance, he was even desperately jealous of him at times.

VOL. II.　　　　　　　　　　　　　　　　E

Mr Tainsh accounted for the stagnant state of his suit by bad luck. He said it was bad luck that checked his progress; and also "that spoony fellow Cameron" had something to do with it, for he was always either in the way, or arriving just at the critical moment; but the real cause did not suggest itself to him: it never occurred to him that he was kept at bay by Eila herself and her wonderful dexterity. Poor Bertrand seemed to have lost all the ground gained at the ball; he hung about Eila, and was rebuffed for doing so; he shunned her presence, and was rebuked for that; he could do nothing right, except, perhaps, once in the twenty-four hours, when she would give him a look, or a word, or a flower, that kept him true to his infatuation.

His feelings towards Mr Tainsh baffle description. To say that he was jealous, is to use a ridiculously inadequate expression. The very thought of the man was becoming madness to him, not merely because Tainsh appeared to be favoured by Eila, but also from a more disinterested feeling that his beautiful ideal was desecrated and outraged by any sort of association with such a terrible embodiment of the common, the prosaic, and the vulgar as his rival appeared to be. Tainsh was a desperately lucky fellow, Bertrand thought, and quite ubiquitous; that is to say, he was desperately sharp and energetic, so that he found time for everything—to transact business in the neighbourhood, to shoot, to fish, to commune with Mr M'Killop, and yet to be always in the way' when Eila was visible. All courage and heart began to fail Bertrand, and he was becoming a mere drifting, drivelling idiot, incapable of spontaneous action. Meantime Eila had a splendid time of it between her two victims. She had got them into such a state of management, that there was no whimsical absurdity she chose to impose upon either, that each was not eager to perform—eager to outstrip the other in performing. She was perpetually seized with a craving for some rare plant or flower, which could only be found among difficult morasses or on the summits of lofty hills; she "suspected that the large mussel found in the river Arvoch was really the pearl-mussel, if one had only time and patience to examine a great number of the shells;" she would give anything in the world for an owl's wing for her hat; and if an eagle's *could* be procured, then, indeed, the cup of her happiness would run over.

These and many similar fancies kept the two men perpetually racing up hills, or hanging over precipices, or wading and groping in river-pools, or stalking imaginary birds and beasts, that offerings might be found for the shrine of their exacting goddess. Pigott was immensely delighted, one evening at nightfall, to come upon Mr Tainsh, crouching, with his gun at full cock, in a clump of trees, and hooting dismally, under the impression that some sympathetic bird of night might be so accommodating as to believe in the simulation, and come to be sacrificed.

"She is admirably cynical, and quite a practical satirist, and it serves the idiots right," chuckled the Captain, as he went away in deep approval.

During these days, Mr Duncanson was doing his possible to make himself agreeable to Morna: he seemed to have an open field —no rival interposed his attentions between Morna and those of the young laird, at all events; and yet he did not appear to make progress any more than Mr Tainsh did. Morna was strangely invisible; she entirely abandoned the pursuit of the gentle art; she never went out on the terrace in the evenings, unless the rest of the party went. A *tête-à-tête* with her seemed to Duncanson to be a thing unattainable. He was angry, he was downcast; his natural disposition was intensely jealous; and without any real point whereon his jealousy could settle satisfactorily, he *was* fiercely jealous now. He spoke to Mrs M'Killop; he all but committed himself irretrievably to that lady, and darkly intimated that he thought he was being humbugged, and found the process unpalatable. Mrs M'Killop did her best to soothe, and at the same time stimulate, and watched all the moves on the double chess-board, with intense anxiety.

Matters stood pretty much in this not very satisfactory condition, when the day fixed for the picnic to Aberlorna arrived. "Everybody," as Pigott put it, "seemed to be in love with everybody, and nobody seemed to like it."

One would have said that he and Mr M'Killop were the only members of the party enjoying a reasonable amount of tranquillity; and therefore, when Mr M'Killop announced his intention of abstaining from the picnic, Pigott was strongly inclined to stay at home also. The rest of the party, however, were so vehement in their expostulations against the decision (an earnestness which Pigott set down as "part of the game"), that he allowed himself to be persuaded, and went, fortifying himself, as he assured Bertrand, "with a double ration of cigars, and committing his body to the deep, in the one hope that everybody else would be violently sea-sick."

The weather did not fall in with this charitable aspiration; and when they reached the sea, after a drive of five miles in the break, nothing could be more inviting than its aspect. A gentle but steady breeze was little more than rippling its surface, and there was the pretty schooner-yacht "lying off and on" about a quarter of a mile from the shore, looking so cheery and inviting, with her snowy sails shining in the sun, her blue pennon fluttering gaily, and her graceful outline giving such suggestions of smooth speed, that even Mrs M'Killop, whose fears had shaped themselves in the direction of Pigott's hopes, looked upon the vessel with a kindly eye.

A bustle upon deck showed that their arrival had been observed, so that the fierce nautical yells and dismal shrieks through a boatswain's whistle, with which Mr Duncanson saluted the craft, and which lasted till the dingey was close to the shore, were rather dramatically pleasing than strictly necessary. The dingey was not nearly large enough to convey the whole party in one trip; so Mr Duncanson, in his quality of host, put off with the first batch, consisting of Mrs M'Killop, Morna, and part of the commissariat under Mr Jenkinson. Arrived at the yacht, he bounded on to the deck with the agility of a corsair, hauled the elder lady painfully up the side, and then, without relinquishing the hand by which he had brought Morna on board, he led her to the taffril, and pointed out the name of the vessel freshly emblazoned in gold—"The Morna."

"What do you think of that, Miss Grant?" he inquired.

"Is that the yacht's name?"

"Of course it is."

"It used to be 'The Dream,' I thought."

"So it was, but I had it altered; my 'Dream,'" he added, with tender significance, "has developed into 'Morna:' do you know who it is named after?"

"Somebody called 'Morna,' I suppose."

"I only know one Morna."

"Me, you mean? but your father may know a great many more; I can't flatter myself that he would call his boat after me—he scarcely knows me."

"He has heard a great deal about you, however; but *I* christened the boat, and it was after you."

"Does your father not object?"

"No, Miss Grant, my father does *not* object; he admires the name as much as I admire the —the—it. Can you guess when I rechristened the yacht?"

"No, I can't; but it was very complimentary of you to call it after me."

"I christened it after you said *that* to me."

"*That*, Mr Duncanson! What?"

"What you said you meant."

"Dear me, how stupid I am! What did I say?"

"About my coming back this week, you know; it made me very happy, and I——"

"Here comes the dingey," said Morna.

The dingey thereupon arriving, Duncanson had to go and play welcoming corsair again; and at last every one was on board, and after an immense amount of rope-hauling, and sail-shifting, and yelling, and whistling, and screaming, and after Mrs M'Killop had been twice nearly knocked overboard by a refractory boom, everything was taut, and the yacht under way, gliding along with wonderful speed, considering the lightness of the breeze. Tainsh was as tenacious as a bull-dog; he never left Eila's side, and soon arranged for her a seat on the leeward side, and took up his position by her. But Bertrand was not going to let him have it all his own way, and immediately placed himself on the other side of the bewitcher. Her manner between the two was a wonder to contemplate.

At one moment it seemed a case of " how happy could I be with either;" the next, a chance word of hers, was making Bertrand tingle with delight, and casting shadows over the lawyer's hard, eager face; and then the next, *vice versâ*.

Both men being fiercely in love and fiercely jealous for the first time in their lives, their cards were lying, face up, on the table before the lady; so that it was easy enough, and no doubt sufficiently delightful, for her to play her own game with the two innocents.

An acute observer might have noticed that, while Tainsh was never snubbed, Bertrand was sometimes not answered at all, or answered almost petulantly; but, on the other hand, he might have observed that, at rare intervals, the latter gentleman was favoured with a look or a tone of a description superior to anything that went in Mr Tainsh's direction.

As an affair of averages, Tainsh certainly had it; but his maximum was far below Bertrand's.

Very effectually, by this disposition of seats, did these two gentlemen cancel each other's efforts, and that was to each the only consolation—cold enough and scant enough comfort truly, unless they were further consoled by contemplating the airy happiness of the divinity at whose feet they were grovelling.

Mr Duncanson being seated with Morna on the other side, Mrs M'Killop was good enough, in the first instance, to bestow her society on Pigott. This appeared to her generalship the most that could be made of the situation. But whether Morna was silent and unresponsive, or whether Mr Duncanson did not find himself so fluent as he had expected, or whether he had something on his mind that required further cogitation, or from whatever cause, the conversation did not go satisfactorily; and at last Duncanson said he would take a turn at the tiller, by Miss Grant's permission. His departure leaving Morna by herself, Pigott transferred his society to her; and this opening a field for new, if minor, combinations to Mrs M'Killop, she straightway joined herself to Eila's group. And here Bertrand lost a point to his adversary by his superior breeding, for he rose and offered his place to Mrs M'Killop, while Tainsh remained as he was. It need scarcely be said that Bertrand's offer was accepted, and as there was no room for a fourth person, Mrs M'Killop really effected his elimination from the group. Thus evicted, Bertrand strolled over to Morna, inwardly consigning Tainsh and his hostess to all sorts of unmentionable retribution.

It had dimly occurred to Bertrand, with all his preoccupation, that Morna's manner was not the same to him as it used to be; and as he sat down at her feet just now he was peculiarly struck with the change. There was a sort of grave reserve—not exactly the reserve of a person who had been offended, but something rather like it—in her manner to him, which, honestly, he did not understand. After all, he said to himself, perhaps she too was only, like him, preoccupied; but about whom? Duncanson, of course. Duncanson? that was so odd, though. Ten days ago she used to abuse him up hill and down dale, and now—well, women were a strange incomprehensible problem, and no mistake. She was a deal too good for Duncanson, though; no mistake about that, either.

"I hope you are enjoying the voyage, Miss Grant," he said, as he seated himself.

"Very much indeed; but I am sorry mamma has been so cruel as to turn you out of your seat."

"Oh, I could not be better placed. You are looking grave: Captain Pigott has been boring you; he *is* a bore. Go away, Pigott, and let me try to cheer Miss Grant up a little."

"I can't say you look too cheerful yourself, Bertrand. Does he, Miss Grant?"

Miss Grant here drew their attention, with a good deal of animation, to a porpoise which was making merry in the offing.

"If you were to sing now, Miss Grant," continued Bertrand, when the porpoise was disposed of, "it would be quite perfect. I never hear you sing now; why is it?"

"I really don't know, Mr Cameron; perhaps you don't ask me to sing; perhaps I don't offer; perhaps we are all too much occupied with other matters—shooting, and so on."

"Will you sing to-day after luncheon?"

"I never sing in the open air."

"Oh, Miss Grant! not even 'The Water-Spirit'?"

Morna replied, deeply blushing, "Never before an audience, and not again even to one auditor: it is bad for the voice, you know," she added, after a pause.

All this time the plungings and buckings of the little ship told that the steerman's attention was not given to the matter in his hand; and, indeed, Duncanson's burning eyes were fastened on the group of which Morna was the centre. He could not distinguish what was being said there, but he could see by Morna's face that something more interesting than chalk or cheese was the topic of conversation. "It must be stopped," he said to himself; and blowing a shrill blast on his horrible whistle, for relief, he was relieved from his post, and descended to stop it accordingly. Whereupon Pigott, whose detestation of Mr Duncanson now almost amounted to a mania, drew off and went forward to the forecastle; and Bertrand, thinking, perhaps, that it was hard to spoil sport, followed him. Whereupon Mrs M'Killop, seeing her dispositions for the moment perfect, rose and followed them. Whereupon Bertrand, magnetised by love and jealousy, at once moved back to her vacant place. Whereupon—but it would be endless to follow the various permutations, the various manœuvres, checks, and counter-checks, of which this deck was the scene without interruption, till the anchor dropped in Aberlorna Bay. "If there was only another fellow here to bet with on the moves, it would be jolly enough," was Pigott's verdict.

They had been coasting along for miles, close to the shore, on the very margin of which, gaunt and treeless mountains rested their rugged feet, with nothing for miles to break the monotony of the landscape; and so, when they rounded a point and turned into the sequestered little bay of Aberlorna, the beauty of the scene which burst upon them was enhanced by contrast and surprise. No contrast could be greater. Channelled in a profound gorge that cleft the mountains with its piny depth, and revealed far away back a vista of cultivated uplands and waving trees, the Lorna came and delivered its sparkling waters to the bay; the embouchure overlooked on one side, as Eila had described it, by the weird old ruin—and, on the other, by the airy elegance of the modern house; the one perched on a grim cliff descending sheerly precipitous to the bay; the other nestling on the highest of a succession of terraces that sloped down with gently-decreasing acclivities, and made their way to the sea amid a triumph of flowers and foliage. On one side, Nature, all unkempt and stern, holding in her brawny arms the rugged relic of the days of eld; on the other,

Art smiling up from her achievements, and, as if half in awe, half in derision, opposing the Beautiful to the Sublime, and the Present to the Past. There was everything about it to touch and awaken Bertrand's poetical instincts. He was gazing for the first time upon the home of his forefathers—those heroic ancestors, those mighty men of valour, whose deeds were engraved on his memory, who lived in his day-dreams as "blameless knights," whose spotless escutcheon was to be a lamp to his path and a light to his feet, as he travelled up the chivalrous ascent to glory.

There was a picturesqueness in his own situation too, thus standing for the first time before the shrine of his hero-worship, that under other circumstances would have entirely captivated his romantic imagination; and, even as it was, the first sight of that venerable tower made his heart swell and his brain begin to teem with troops of thick-coming fancies; but Eila was by his side, and, at the sound of her voice, his ancestors went quietly back to sleep in their vault in the kirk of Aberlorna.

"Did I describe it well? is it not beautiful?" said the enchantress.

"It is indeed beautiful; but as I should always associate it with your description—with the sound of your voice," he added, dropping his own, "it would appear perfect to me with half its charms."

"Look, Miss Eila," said Tainsh; "look at that lowest terrace; that's my doing—I made it without consulting Sir Roland."

"It must have looked unfinished without it, I think."

"Just that; it did. I think I have got the place in fair order now; but I suspect I'll have to cut down a lot of these old trees on the other side."

Tainsh, speaking as the factor, adopted an especially proprietary tone, intended to jar upon, and snub, Bertrand, who said—

"Pray don't cut any of the wood on that side. I am sure Sir Roland would not approve. It would spoil the place."

"Well, you see, if I get *carte-blanche* I must use my own discretion; when Sir Roland intrusts you with these matters, of course I will listen to your opinion."

"You never got *carte-blanche* to the extent you propose to go. I protest against your touching the wood on that side. I warn you not to do it. And I shall write to Sir Roland."

Then for a second or two the rivals glared at each other in silence.

"I vow it puts me monstrously in mind of Tillywheesle—it always did," cried Mrs M'Killop to Pigott.

"I would pull down that rickety old ruin," said Duncanson, "and add another story to the new house; it does not seem big enough for a gentleman to live in."

"You would make it look like a cotton-mill if you did," remarked Pigott; "which would be all very well for the residence of a cotton lord, but not of a gentleman."

And when every one had pronounced upon the subject after his kind, the disembarkation began; and here matters so fell out—what between Tainsh's tenacity, and Mrs M'Killop's astuteness, and Duncanson's control of the situation—that the boat, on its first trip, conveyed Eila, Tainsh, and the commissariat to land. On arriving there, it was, according to arrangement, run ashore on the left bank of the little stream, and there the butler and the provisions were landed; but Eila expressing a wish to get an upward view of the ruin from the foot of the cliff, she and Mr Tainsh were landed on the other side; and the dingey went back and performed its two other trips, landing its passengers successfully on the left bank, and, that accomplished, returning to the yacht. Thus it came about, that when Eila had satisfied herself with the view, and she and Tainsh returned to the bank of the stream, they found that the party had gone away inland, believing them to be in front; that the dingey had disappeared; and that they had no means of crossing the stream at that point to rejoin them.

"It is most provoking," said Eila; "we shall be obliged to climb all the way up by the old castle and reach them by the bridge."

But Tainsh's heart beat high with joy and excitement. He blessed the absence of the dingey, he blessed the intervening Lorna, he blessed the length of the ascent. He felt that his opportunity had come, and he was not the man to let it slip. And thus while Bertrand was tearing like a maniac up the ascent on the other side, straining anxious eyes to get a glimpse of the bewitcher, behold her slowly climbing the reverse bank, undisputedly in the hands of the Philistine, and that Philistine quite alive to his advantage, and determined to make the best of it.

CHAPTER XV.

THE path which led up to the old castle proved to be both narrow and steep, circumstances which enforced a slow rate of progress on the climbers, and at the same time made it expedient that one should precede the other. This was most tantalising to Mr Tainsh, who felt that, in such a position, it was impossible for him to say what he had to say—what he had quite resolved to say—and that golden moments were slipping by, perhaps to leave an insufficient margin of time, when they had reached the summit, before an interruption took place. With feverish irritation, therefore, he observed the leisurely way in which Eila conducted the march, pausing now and then to comment upon the scenery, but making no remark that could in any way form a basis for the commencement of his operations.

Tainsh, by the by, had a vague notion that, in all well-regulated proposals, a kneeling scene was *de rigueur*, and if it had not been for this, he might perhaps have seized the opportunity of one of Eila's halts to plunge *in medias res*. But how kneel and employ proper oratorical action on a narrow shelf overhanging a precipice of many hundred feet? It was not to be thought of; and so he plodded after Eila in silent impatience, scanning with anxious eyes, now the summit of the cliff, now the other side of the glen where he knew the party would be in quest of them.

At length the ascent was achieved, and Eila accepted Mr Tainsh's suggestion that they should sit down and rest awhile.

Behold them, then, seated on a small tablet of rock, facing the sea, shadowed by the umbrage of the venerable oaks, and with ample room and verge enough for Mr Tainsh to kneel, oratorise, stand on his head, and be as ridiculous and acrobatic as he pleased.

"Just the place for it," thought Tainsh; "here goes!" and then he began,—"Miss M'Killop, in a scene like this—in scenery like this, the heart of man is naturally elevated." Here he paused.

"Oh yes, indeed it is," replied Eila; "there is something about the antique that is very inspiring, and there is something in this grand prospect—in these lights and shadows on the sea, in these sombre woods and rugged cliffs—that does, as you say, elevate the heart. The odd thing is that Sir Roland does not appreciate the place. I suspect Mr Cameron will, when he succeeds to it; he will succeed to it, of course?"

"Yes," stammered Tainsh, "oh yes; humanly speaking, he will—that is, I suspect so, if his uncle doesn't marry."

"But then he is so old."

"Yes, he is elderly, of course. Sitting in scenes like these, Miss Eila, with the heart thus elevated, my brain at this moment becomes dizzy."

"Oh, then, pray let us get farther back; some people, I know, cannot bear to be near a precipice. I don't understand the feeling myself. You feel inclined to throw yourself over, don't you?" and she rose as if to change her position.

"Please sit still, Miss M'Killop; it was of a mental dizziness I spoke."

"Oh! nothing to do with the precipice?"

"Nothing to do with *that* precipice at all. My brain, as I was going to say, becomes dizzy—beauty thrilling it in all its fibres—beauty intoxicating, bewildering——."

"You are quite a poet, Mr Tainsh; if you are also an artist, I wish you would sketch the bay for me. I have everything here; will you?"

"I am sorry I cannot. I am no artist—no poet either; but certain feelings, they say, make poets of the dullest of mankind."

"Fine scenery has made many poets, I believe."

"And female loveliness, Miss M'Killop."

"Do you think so?"

"Yes; and under the influence of the two combined, as I am at this moment, he would indeed be prosaic who did not feel some poetical inspiration."

"Suppose you write some verses; I promise to keep perfectly quiet."

"That is exactly what I don't wish. No, I will not—I could never—express in writing what I feel at this moment."

"What *is* that sea-gull about?" exclaimed Eila, with great earnestness, pointing to a bird which was fishing in the bay below. Tainsh smothered an uncivil remark about the gull, and went on poetically, "I sometimes wish I had the wings of a bird."

"I would I were a bird," hummed Eila, gaily, adding, "Are you fond of the Christy Minstrels?"

Her sudden levity rather baffled Mr Tainsh's earnestness.

"No—yes—they are very good—sometimes. That bird down there," he continued, "is happier than I am, Miss Eila. He has his hunger, and he satisfies it. I, too, have my hunger——"

"Oh, then," cried Eila, "pray don't let us stay any longer here! I am quite rested; and besides, I am beginning to feel hungry too, so let us go and look for the luncheon; it won't come to us, I suspect. After all, that bird has inspired you with an idea much more useful than poetical images."

"Ah! do not misinterpret me; I spoke of a hunger of the soul."

"Really, Mr Tainsh, you mix your metaphors, your prose, and your poetry so strangely, that you *are* a little incomprehensible. You want to throw yourself over a precipice, you want to fly away with the bird's wings, and then you want to eat his dinner, and then—then—what is it next?"

The next step came unexpectedly enough, for, at this rather inopportune juncture, Mr Tainsh put an end to all further doubt or skirmishing, by plunging down upon his knees in front of Eila.

"Eila! I love, I adore you!" he exclaimed, clasping his hands, and bending forward in the attitude accepted on the stage as that of the shipwrecked mariner, just washed ashore by the "fer-endly billows."

A quick gleam of some emotion passed across the lady's face, and there was a sudden compression of the lips which might have indicated suppressed mirth under circumstances of less solemn interest. In an instant, however, and whatever the emotion may have been, her face was composed into an expression of grief and compassion. Her beautiful eyes were opened wide, and gazed on her suitor through a sudden mist of impending tears.

"Rise, Mr Tainsh!" she cried—"rise up;

it is unworthy of you or of any man to kneel before a silly girl like me."

"I will not rise," cried Tainsh, recklessly, "until you grant the prayer of my heart. Give me, oh, give me, what a thousand words, a thousand looks, a thousand other symptoms, lead me to hope that I may—I must—have! —give me the verbal assurance of your love."

"Mr Tainsh, is it possible you are in earnest, or this only a pleasantry—an ill-judged one, I must say? or——"

"I am as solemnly in earnest as a man can be, whose whole happiness is hanging on a word."

"Why did I not see—why did I not suspect —understand this before? You are the last person I should have expected to profess such sentiments; but my surprise is nothing to the pain and regret I feel for having misunderstood you, for having perhaps mis——"

"Say no more on that head, Eila—only answer me this; may I hope that my love is not utterly unrequited?"

Eila's answer was, "Oh no, no, Mr Tainsh! you have been deceiving yourself as to my sentiments."

N.B.—Double negatives ought to be avoided when a clear understanding is really desired.

"On the contrary, Eila, I have read your heart; I have often felt that it was mine. Doubts and fears have arisen at times, but I forget them all in the supreme happiness of this avowal—all—all."

"Oh! listen to me, Mr Tainsh; I can never forgive myself——"

"Banish all such regrets and recriminations, adorable Eila, as I banish the recollection of them; and now you know me in my true character as your lover, let us resign ourselves to the joy of the moment. Give free play to your affection; believe me it is requited fourfold."

He showed symptoms of abandoning the attitude of the mariner for one of a more aggressive description, but Eila started back with so much vivacity that he subsided into his nautical *pose* again, while she cried, "If you will always interrupt and misunderstand me, how can I set you right, Mr Tainsh? You are only aggravating my pain and your own by prolonging this scene. Understand me once for all, when I say that you have mistaken my sentiments as entirely as I appear to have misunderstood yours. Mine have all along been those of sincere friendship and respect, but nothing more; and my regret, my deep regret, is, that my manner—too familiar and intimate, perhaps—may have led you to interpret them otherwise."

"Which of us is dreaming?" said Tainsh, hazily, passing his hand across his forehead.

"Ah! dear Mr Tainsh," said Eila, in a tone of infinite gentleness and sympathy, "it grieves me to the heart to see you so distressed, and for such an unworthy cause. Look on this—this fancy for me, as a dream; and may you find happiness from some better and more substantial cause."

"It is all dark and incomprehensible to me," murmured Mr Tainsh, who indeed appeared to be in a state of complete bewilderment. "Am I to understand that you do *not* love me?"

"I greatly like, esteem, respect you, Mr Tainsh, as a valued friend."

"But as a lover you spurn, reject, despise me?"

"Not so; you put harsh words into my mouth; it is not fair. I say nothing of the sort; all I say is that our union is impossible."

"The feelings you have named," cried Tainsh, again lighted up with hope, "what are they but the elements of which love is made up? It is you, believe me, Eila, who have deceived yourself; with such feelings as you express, our union is *not* impossible, but the contrary. Do not finally cheat your heart. Marry me, Eila, and take my word for it, that your affection will be given with your hand."

"Mr Tainsh, it appears to me that you pretend to know more of my feelings than I do myself."

"In this case I am certain that it is so. I am led to understand that the hurry and surprise attending such proposals are so confusing to the recipient, that they are often mechanically refused, and love and happiness sacrificed for ever. A little self-examination is often necessary to let the heart discover how it stands. So take till to-morrow, and answer me then. I am not afraid to let you analyse your feelings — to let you investigate this liking, this esteem, this respect."

"To-morrow my answer would be exactly the same—that our union is impossible."

"No doubt it appears so to you now; take a week, then."

"It would be useless."

"A month—a year."

"I tell you once for all, that a century would not alter my decision."

"You deceive yourself, you deceive yourself, believe me!" cried Mr Tainsh, in the same tone of superior intelligence. "Now, before we part, let me hear you say, 'Alexander, my feelings are perplexed; I will examine them honestly, however, and see whether this liking, this esteem, this respect, do not amount, after all, to love. Alexander, I will try to love you.'"

"Mr Tainsh——"

"Alexander," substituted the factor.

Eila was too angry, by this time, to laugh at the uncouth tenacity displayed by her lover, and the perverse incredulity with which he received all her assurances of indifference; and grievous though it may be to a certain school of ladies, of whose idiosyncrasies, in this respect, Eila certainly partook, to abridge the feline joy of torturing their victims with alternations of fear and hope, and to part finally with even an indifferent or distasteful lover — grievous though this may have been to her, her indignation forced her to make the sacrifice. Fortunate for all parties, for otherwise the discussion might have been going on to this hour; it is certain that Tainsh's kneecaps (he was still kneeling) would have given way sooner than his resolute determination to believe in Eila's love, or, at least, to argue her into a belief of it.

"Mr Tainsh," cried the young lady, "I will *not* be treated like a child; and as you will not bring this singular conversation to a close, I must do so by leaving you. I can no longer endure it. I think I have spoken as plainly as consideration for your feelings would allow me; I must say you show little delicacy or consideration for mine; and now I shall leave you: not another word, I beg" (as Tainsh was about to speak); "my answer is perfectly final and distinct, and, if you will have it broadly, it is 'No.'" Hereupon Mr Tainsh rose swiftly to his feet. He had been unused to failure in his undertakings; his creed was, that energy, tenacity, and power of will are irresistible forces; an admirable creed in most departments of human endeavour; but Tainsh was testing its soundness in one perfectly unfamiliar to him—in one where axioms are impossible, where analogy fails, and where even very special experience is quite an unreliable guide. It is questionable whether the disappointment of his hopes as a lover, was anything like so poignant a feeling as the conviction that he had been foiled in a purpose which he had deliberately set himself to compass. The two combined certainly worked him into a state of complete exasperation; and he now addressed Eila in a strain of vehement recrimination, betraying all the coarseness of mind and vulgarity of manner which, even under favourable circumstances, revealed themselves through a veneering of better things.

"Then," he cried, "I have been duped and befooled! What have all these soft looks and sweet speeches been? So many frauds and falsehoods. Don't try to humbug me with this trash about friendship. It was not friendship you were playing at. The game you have been playing is not one a friend would have played. You have been using me — that's about it—for your own purposes; and if they were gained, what were my feelings to you? The whole thing is clear to me now; I remember who has been dangling about you. You have shown great skill; you have thrown dust in my eyes very successfully; you must be a practised hand at a double game. And that other fool—his attentions were distasteful too, perhaps? Oh no, that won't do. He is to be something more than a friend, I should say; and I have been used, to bring him up to the scratch. I shall feel shame to my dying day that I have been tricked and played with, all to serve the purpose of a vain, shallow-hearted girl. Well, I wish you joy of Mr Bertrand Cameron. Perhaps you would like to get a little private intelligence about the estate, before you finally decide whether he is to be a *friend* or—what shall I say ?—a speculation? One can never be too careful in money transactions."

Mr Tainsh spoke with so much energy that Eila had not a chance of interrupting him, till he paused for sheer lack of breath; nor could she make her escape, for he stood in front of her, barring the path, with vehement gesticulations. Now, however, with flashing eyes, in which tears, from no tender fountain, trembled, and in a voice that shook with passion, she replied—

"I, too, shall feel shame to my dying day that I have admitted to any kind of intimacy such a—such a person as you are—capable of using such language to a lady—to any woman. Your vulgarity, of course, I have known, all along; that, one could forgive, for it was your birthright. But this dastardly insolence—— I wonder you don't strike me; it would not be at all more insulting, or more unmanly than your words. And now let me pass, sir. I presume, since you have *not* struck me, that you will not venture to detain me by force," for Mr Tainsh, with his arms extended to give oratorical action to some new diatribe, looked as though he were attempting to pen her in to the platform where they had been seated. Thus were the two confronting each other; Tainsh pale with passion, his eyes dilated, his uncovered head (for his hat had fallen off at the kneeling scene) thrust forward as if to accelerate his fierce utterance, and his arms wildly brandished in the air; Eila, on the other hand, haughty and erect, her beautiful eyes blazing through indignant tears, and one hand slightly moved with a contemptuous gesture; — thus were they confronting each other, when, on a ledge above, suddenly appeared four spectators. These were Mrs M'Killop, Morna, Bertrand, and Duncanson. The respective attitudes of the couple below were observed by this group; and although it was but for an instant, and although the accents in which their dialogue was being conducted were but indistinctly heard, Mrs M'Killop instantly grasped the real state of the case, and instantly raised her voice to warn those below that they *were* observed.

"Eila! Eila! Eila!"

Eila looked quickly up; her self-possession returned on the moment; she softened her attitude off at once into one of careless *abandon*; and, still looking up to the party above, rapidly whispered to Tainsh, almost below her breath—

"For your own sake, I should recommend you to help me to pass this off as if there was nothing in it." Then raising her voice: "Ah! you have found us at last; we were just on the point of starting to look for you." Then, again in a whisper, to Tainsh: "Put your hat on, and try not to look so utterly ridiculous."

Now when a man feels himself to be looking utterly ridiculous, it does not usually mend matters to assure him that such is the case, or to beg him to assume a different appearance; and the device was, in this instance, decidedly unsuccessful. In his then exasperated state, nothing but the instinct of self-preservation (from ridicule) would have induced Mr Tainsh to listen to any suggestion of Eila's; but *it* did: and thus being discovered in the attitude of a spread-eagle—a peculiar one, to say the least of it, in which to carry on a quiet *tête-à-tête*—his method of appearing more easy and natural was to exchange it for that of the gorged vulture attempting to rise from the earth, with the slow and solemn wing-flapping action appropriate to that bird and to the effort; looking up, the while, at the new arrivals with what was intended for an easy smile, but which, if it could have been set up to auction as a dramatic scowl, would have fetched a long price in the profession. Thus scowling and flapping, he made his way to his hat, and put it on with a ferocious jauntiness ; and if ever there had been a chance of the scene passing off as a commonplace *tableau* in a commonplace interview, poor Tainsh's efforts not "to look utterly ridiculous" would have entirely annihilated it.

The hat reclaimed, they joined the party above, to whom Eila made a statement purporting to detail their proceedings, and involving quite an interesting *précis* of a tale which Mr Tainsh was represented (much to his surprise) to have told with great spirit and appropriate action, resulting in his hatless condition at its close. Then they all turned in quest of the luncheon, which was found not far off under charge of the butler, who, with Pigott's assistance, was anxiously compounding some cunning drink, under the greenwood tree.

The meal itself could not be said to pass off cheerily. In addition to the *gêne* of one sullen, silent, unhappy presence (for Tainsh's dramatic effort on the cliff was not to be sustained), there was a certain awkward restraint observable in the rest of the party, all, save the unconscious Pigott, more or less engrossed with the episode which they had interrupted. Eila, it is true, did her best, by more than usual vivacity, to keep things going, but in vain. Curious, furtive glances, now at Tainsh, now at her, were the only reward of her efforts; and the difficulty of coping with protracted and recurring pauses, made her and every one else thankful when the luncheon could, without absolute outrage to the theory that it was a convivial occasion, be pronounced at an end.

A stroll to see the ruins was then proposed, and they started off *en masse*. That formation, however, did not long subsist; very soon the party was broken up into couples, of which Tainsh and Mrs M'Killop naturally were one, Morna and Duncanson another, while Eila found herself under the escort of our two friends. The adage that "three is no company" is a sound one under certain circumstances. Pigott thought it applicable to the present occasion, and he very soon detached himself from his companions, returning to the beach to await the hour of departure with what patience he might command, and very thankful for the foresight which had suggested a double ration of cigars. We are not going to follow these several couples, or listen to their conversation as they roamed through the woods and scrambled among the rocks and ruins; suffice it for the present to say that Pigott's patience was sorely tried. Mrs M'Killop and Mr Tainsh, indeed, returned in a reasonable time; but their society was neither amusing in itself, nor did their arrival advance the moment of departure. As for the others, it seemed as if they would never come. In vain were the two gentlemen despatched to seek and shout through the woods; and in vain did Mrs M'Killop querulously call upon some invisible power to explain "what, in the name of wonder, they could mean" by their prolonged absence.

Their patience was wellnigh exhausted, and Pigott was beginning to suggest the propriety of attempting to take up transport and proceed home overland, when at last the loiterers *did* come, all together, all silent, and all unmoved by the reproachful questions of their friends.

There was not much time for parley, however, as the hour was late, and the breeze might fail; so, without any of the morning's manœuvres, the re-embarkation was effected as quickly as possible. In the morning, if the party had not been a very happy or harmonious one, at least there had been some spirit and energy about it; but now what had come over them all? Mute was the boatswain's whistle; vanished the elastic vigour of the corsair; strategy was dormant; Mrs M'Killop motionless, and even dumb: there were neither permutations nor combinations; the units of the party sat apart; there was a gloomy silence. Bertrand and Eila, indeed, sat together: why did they not speak? Why was Bertrand throwing away his chances? The sky, too, had turned leaden and sad, the air cold and raw; and the breeze, now gusty and squalliferous, whistled through the rigging of the "Morna" with shrill and shrewish tones, as if interpreting the spirit that reigned upon her deck.

All were relieved when the *triste* passage came to an end. It was late; it was dark; no one wanted anything to eat. So the ladies went to bed funereally; Tainsh and Duncanson repaired sullenly to the smoking-room; while Pigott and Bertrand betook themselves to their own sanctum, whither let us follow them, as to the brightest and cheeriest room in the house.

CHAPTER XVI.

"I REMARKED this morning," said Pigott, when they were seated by their own fireside,—"I remarked this morning, when we were outward bound, that everybody seemed to be in love with everybody, and nobody seemed to like it. To-night I remark of the homeward voyage, that everybody seemed to be out of love with everybody, without any happier results. What does it all mean? What has happened? What is it, Bertrand? Has every one gone mad but old M'Killop and I? You're one of the *dramatis personæ;* unriddle me the mystery, if you please."

"Well, Pigott," said Bertrand, staring dreamily into the fire, "a good many things have happened to-day, I suspect."

"A shrewd suspicion, and I share it; but I am self-supporting in that line. I want something else,—experiences—facts, at least. Give me some."

"I'm awfully happy, Pigott," murmured Bertrand.

"You must be own brother to Mark Tapley, then. A day like this would have tried even his philosophy beyond endurance, I should say."

"Ah! you don't know," replied Bertrand, absently; and then, in an undertone to himself, "Oh! terque, quaterque beatus!"

Pigott stared at his friend, and exclaimed, "Mad, and speaking with tongues! What next?"

"Terque, quaterque beatus!"

"Well, I can't say you look it. Are all the rest of you in the same state of death's-head-and-cross-bones beatitude? Tainsh, for instance?"

"Tainsh! I should like to see the ruffian hanged, drawn, and quartered," shouted Bertrand, with something more even than his old energy.

"By all manner of means," said Pigott; "terque quaterque, if you please; and if you like to include Duncanson, I am with you there very especially. But you'll spare the ladies, I hope?"

"Don't be a fool. I spoke of Tainsh, the scoundrel, the villain!"

"Well, well, granted: Tainsh be hanged; and what next?"

"You've no idea what a villain Tainsh is, Pigott."

"To tell you the truth, it doesn't tax my imaginative powers very heavily to form a conception. But what has he been doing?"

"I think I shall horsewhip him; I think I *must* horsewhip him."

"Do; and when you *are* about that sort of thing, perhaps, as a special favour to me, you wouldn't mind licking Duncanson too."

"I'm not in joke, I assure you."

"No more am I; but what has Tainsh been about?"

"That involves the whole story."

"Confound the fellow! let us *have* the whole story, then."

"Well, Tainsh has grossly insulted Miss M'Killop."

"No!"

"Grossly."

"Horrible! how?"

"Why, would you believe it? he actually had the outrageous insolence to propose to her to-day."

"Good heavens, how very shocking!—the heart of man is desperately wicked, beyond a question."

"Now, Pigott, I'm not in the humour for trifling."

"My dear fellow, who *is* trifling? So Tainsh proposed, did he? I thought he would; but I'll lay short odds she didn't accept him."

"Pigott, do you wish to insult *me?*" cried Bertrand, starting from his chair.

"Heaven forbid! if you'll only tell me how to avoid it. To clear the atmosphere, I've freely assented to every proposition you have made about Tainsh; and if you'll only explain how Miss M'Killop's acceptance or refusal of him is supposed to insult you, I'll take uncommon good care to say the right thing."

"I don't wish to be treated like a child."

"Oh, this is getting too tiresome: if you don't want to be treated like a child, try to speak like a man, and let us have done with this maundering nonsense. Why should Tainsh's proposal be an insult to the lady? and, in the name of common-sense, how could her supposed acceptance be an insult to *you?* You appear to me to be taking leave of your senses altogether, Bertrand."

"Of course he might propose—although, in my opinion, it was consummate impertinence; but if you would, for once—only for once—as a special favour, allow me to speak without interrupting me, I would explain."

"Go on, then."

"Well, it wasn't so much the proposal, as the way he received her answer, that was outrageous; and for which I must call him to account."

"*You*, Bertrand?"

"Yes, *I*, Pigott."

"But, bless me! what is it to you? how do you know about it? surely you weren't present?"

"No, nor yet eaves-dropping. Listen; before luncheon we all came upon Miss M'Killop and Tainsh—suddenly. She was looking like —like what the poets call a Pythoness——"

"Variety of the sea-serpent," interpolated Pigott.

"Silence! She was looking as I say, and he was looking like the villain he is, only foiled, and sold, and exasperated. I could see with half an eye that we had come at a serious crisis; but it passed off as if nothing had happened. Eila showed such tact. But Tainsh was as white as a sheet, and as silent as could be; didn't you notice him at luncheon? mooning and giving crooked answers, and upsetting things?"

"I certainly had my suspicions."

"Well, after luncheon, if you remember, you joined her and me for a bit; and it wasn't lively, was it?"

"Not strictly speaking lively—no."

"And then you sheered off?"

"I 'saved myself,' as the French express it."

"But, even after you had gone, she continued silent and preoccupied."

"I wasn't the bore, then?"

"Oh no; so I said to her frankly, after a while, 'You are silent, Miss M'Killop, and I fear something has annoyed you: can I be of any use?' I meant, could I do anything to —to—do away with her annoyance. And she said, 'I *am* annoyed—and more than that a great deal, for I have been grievously insulted; but you must not ask me about it, for it is a subject that cannot possibly be discussed between you and me. Are you fond of ferns?' But I wouldn't turn the subject, and said, 'You may tell me or not, as you please, but I am certain I know who the insulter is, and I'll just have the honour of going and throwing him over the precipice.' She thought I was going on the instant, for she stopped and clasped my arm with both her hands, and implored me, for her sake, not to do so. What divine eyes she has, to be sure! Do you remember the Madonna at Dresden?"

"No, I don't; go on with your story."

"Of course I didn't go then; and she said, 'I didn't think you were such a Don Quixote.' 'I am not a Don Quixote,' I replied; 'he fought for and with visions, delusions, and phantasies.' 'And you?' she said. 'And I,' I replied, 'would fight and would die for you, who are not a vision, nor a delusion, nor a phantasy.' 'I did not dream that I was so highly honoured,' she answered. 'I hope you are not mocking me, Miss M'Killop,' I said.

'Mocking you!' she cried; 'do you think I have no gratitude? You are too good, too kind, to feel such interest in one who is, after all, little more than a stranger.' Then," said Bertrand, rising up in the excitement of his narration,—" then I cried out to her that if she was a stranger to me, so was the heart that beat in my breast—so was every thought that passed through my mind—so was every bright and beautiful thing in nature; for to me she was the soul, the divine inspiring principle, that lent them all their life and all their enchantment. 'Mr Cameron,' she said, looking deeply astonished and almost frightened, for I was carried away with my excitement—'what is this?' 'It is what men call "Love,"' I cried: 'but that cannot describe it; for if all the love that all mankind have felt before, were condensed into one consummate passion, it would be tame and cold indifference compared with mine for you.'"

"Not so bad—really not half so bad for a beginner," said Pigott. "Do you know, Bertrand, you looked rather like the picture of Kemble at 'the Garrick' when you said that just now?"

Bertrand was far too much rapt to notice this calm interruption, and he went on—" I offered her my heart, I offered her my devotion, I offered her my life."

"And she took them—all three, I'll bet long odds ?"

" Silence ! how dare you ? She admitted that I was not indifferent to her, but that Tainsh had proposed to her that morning, and that when she rejected his audacious and insulting proposal, he had employed language, reproaches, insinuations, that had almost overwhelmed her. One of these insinuations was so painful, and, at the same time, so closely connected with my declaration, that she must decline, at whatever sacrifice of personal happiness, to receive that declaration. 'What was it ?' I inquired. And then she told me, with such childlike simplicity, that this monster had actually insinuated that she had been running after me, and playing him to bring me on ! The idea was so ludicrous that I fairly laughed outright at it : that reassured her a little ; and then I pointed out to her the wrong that she would do to us both, if she allowed the venomous words of a disappointed wretch like that, to separate two hearts which loved each other so fondly. After a long time she agreed to take this view of it; and we had an hour together, in which the bliss of ten lifetimes seemed to be concentrated."

"You're engaged to her, then?" asked Pigott, as if the question was a most trivial commonplace.

"Completely," replied his friend. "You take it pretty coolly, I must say; you don't seem to be the least astonished."

"I never am, you know; and even if I ever was, I don't think this would be likely to astonish me."

"You foresaw it?"

"Rather."

"Well, I didn't; I thought I would try, of course; but as to my success, that was all a matter of perfect doubt. I'm so utterly unworthy of her."

"Humph!"

"What do you mean by 'Humph'?"

"Incipient bronchitis, I fear."

"You don't congratulate me."

"I do."

"Give me your hand, and show a little

heartiness. Every one likes sympathy in such cases ; don't be an oyster."

" I *am* rather an oyster by nature, Bertrand," said Pigott, giving his hand with, for him, a good deal of kindliness ; " but depend upon it, I am not so about your affairs ; and I am sure I wish you happiness with all my heart."

" And don't you think I'm the luckiest dog in the world ? "

" Ahem ! Well—no—scarcely."

" What do you mean, Pigott ? "

" Every man has a right to his opinion, you know. Now, I look on single blessedness as the happiest state ; and therefore I can't look upon a man qualifying for the other event, as the happiest of mortals."

" Well, but my choice—my *fiancée*—is she not an angel ? "

" These are the kind of terms, Bertrand, that always make me very ill ; please use them to-night even, as sparingly as possible, like a good fellow. Your *fiancée* is a remarkably pretty girl, and both clever and agreeable. I know that ; but I haven't the remotest conception of what an angel is like, any more than I have of the Pythoness you compared her to before."

"What a crotchety, prosaic old bird you are! But I've been forgetting, as well I might—though I have hardly realised my happiness yet—I've been forgetting about Tainsh. It is clearly my part to call him to account."

" Take my advice, and let Tainsh alone."

"Oh no; I could not sleep to-night without settling with him."

" The conqueror, in the hour of victory, can afford to be merciful."

"Very true ; but, at all events, he is entitled to prescribe the conditions of his mercy. Tainsh must apologise, or come out, or be horse-whipped."

"By heavens, Bertrand! you should have been an Irishman. This is the way you would break the news of your betrothal to the lady's parents. Fancy the *tableau!* Hour—midnight; scene—the smoking-room. Yells are heard. Concourse of old M'Killop and the servants. Tainsh discovered, weltering in his blood, among heaps of broken furniture ; you dancing a war-dance over him. Father of *fiancée* asks what these things mean. You (brandishing leg of table, dripping with factor's gore) exclaim, 'Behold the miscreant who insulted your daughter!—who, by the by, is engaged to me—have the goodness to have his carcass flung out of doors; and now, old man, for your blessing!' As a method of entering a family, it certainly has the merit of originality."

"It is all very fine to make a joke of serious matters; easy enough, too, for those who have no feeling; but, I think, even you might see that this is a case where either an apology, or the usual alternative, is absolutely necessary, and where I am clearly the person to demand or to inflict."

"Now, really, my dear Bertrand, you are too childish. Sleep over the matter, at all events; and then, when you are acknowledged as Miss M'Killop's betrothed publicly, you may perhaps with less absurdity pull up Mr Tainsh! But, if you take my advice, you will let the thing alone, and not make a scandal—which is always unpleasant for a lady. After all, the man is a vulgar snob. He was bitterly disappointed, and he lost his temper—you don't know what aggravation he may have had—and being angry, he spoke after his kind."

"I'll teach him to speak after his kind to his own kind, for the future. I'm quite resolved; and I'll go down now, and get it off my mind. Though Eila did not wish me to throw him over the precipice, she must clearly expect me to take some steps in the matter. No girl of spirit could allow such an outrage to pass."

"You had better let me go for you, then," suggested Pigott, "if you *must* act in the matter."

"That would not do at present. If further steps are necessary, I shall, of course, have to ask for your assistance; and now I'm off."

"Well," said Pigott, "if you will be an idiot, at all events promise me one thing—that you won't take to hammering Tainsh to-night, and make a row and a scene in this house."

"I won't, unless the course of the interview positively compels me to deal with him on the spot."

"What, Bertrand! you — a gentleman — a chivalrous high-bred lover—make a low disturbance, and a scene fit for a St Giles's pothouse, in the house where your beautiful betrothed is sleeping! For shame!"

"You're right, Pigott; and I promise you I won't lay a finger on him to-night, or in this house. If it is necessary, I shall merely warn him what is to happen, and tell him in the mean time to consider himself hammered."

"How well you are up in all sorts of Paddiana! But I am glad you are decided not to execute him on the spot. Stick to your decision."

"I will;" and Bertrand left the room.

In the smoking-room, where Tainsh and Duncanson sat together, the conversation did not, by any means, flow so freely as it had been doing in the room above. Gloom and embarrassment sat on the countenances of both gentlemen. Each, from time to time, regarded the other with the furtive air of a man who has a secret, who half suspects that his neighbour is cognisant of it, and who is in doubt whether or not it would be better to abandon reserve, and make a confidant, as the less of two evils. Tainsh, as we have seen, had good reason for this feeling. His exhibition on the cliff would not bear reflecting upon; the more he thought of it the more he feared that his appearance, gestures, and subsequent demeanour must have revealed to all observers the story of his humiliation. Tainsh had good reason ;— but Duncanson? We have seen, we have heard, nothing of his day's proceedings that could lead us or Tainsh to suspect that anything very special had happened to him. He had sulked and brooded all the way home, to be sure, but then he was always sulking and brooding—there was nothing in that. Tainsh could know nothing more about him. There are, however, many men whose egotism would seem to carry them the length of thinking that anything specially affecting themselves — particularly to their detriment — is necessarily unfolded to the world at large, by some supernatural revelation. Duncanson was of this class; and, as he sat smoking and casting his queer glances at Tainsh, his thought was the exact counterpart of the thought of his companion, whose smoke mingled with his, and whose queer glances crossed swords, as it were, with his own—and that thought was, "Does he know, does he suspect, the grief I have come to?"

It is the tritest of observations, that certain classes of events, not merely misfortunes, never come singly, but, in their occurrences and recurrences, present themselves in groups; and foremost among such, as will probably be admitted, stand those connected with matrimony. Who has not in his recollection some such instance as a family of, say four or five spinster sisters, who remained (unwillingly) in blessed celibacy till the most sanguine backer shook his head, and even the enemy grew tired of pointing the finger of scorn; and yet, when a turn came at last, and one of the virgin band did change her condition, lo and behold! all the rest almost tripped over each other in the tumultuous rapidity with which they followed to the altar? Who has not remarked the phenomenon of a matrimonial season, when all one's friends appear to fall in love and get married *en masse?* as also the phenomenon of a celibate season, when the market is absolutely stagnant, when inexorably there are "no takers," when the charm of the charmer casts its glamour in vain, and the strategist's polished skill is wasted on futile combinations?

These phenomena are as unaccountable as cholera or rinderpest, the disease in grouse or in potatoes; but we are all perfectly satisfied of their existence; and therefore no one need feel surprise when we account for Mr Duncanson's peculiar demeanour in the smoking-room by announcing, that he too had, on this day, been putting his fate and his desert to the test, and with results eminently unsatisfactory to himself. To make a long story short, Morna had refused Mr Duncanson, at which surely all her friends must rejoice.

We are not going to reproduce here the scene as it occurred; the airy self-confidence with which the swain addressed himself to his task; the skill of fence displayed by the lady in her anxiety to save him from rushing on his fate; the graceful rhetoric with which he urged his suit, and the angry surprise with which he received his rebuff. All these things must be imagined. He did not require to be argued into the belief that he was refused, like Mr Tainsh. At the first hint of a negative, his vanity and temper rose; he hastily picked up the handkerchief which he had thrown, and, after briefly assuring Miss Grant that she would probably live to repent her folly, relapsed into the sullen silence in which we find him in the smoking-room. A light-hearted outsider would have gone into fits of laughter admitted to the spectacle of these two men, as they sat mute and scowling among their unmollifying tobacco-smoke. The silence was at last broken by Duncanson, who remarked, tentatively—

"You seem out of spirits to-night, Tainsh."

"It was on the tip of my tongue to say the same of you, Duncanson," was the eager reply.

"Really? It was not a very successful day, was it? deuced slow, I thought."

"A little slow, perhaps," replied Tainsh, wishing that in one respect he himself had been a little slower.

"I don't think the women liked it," continued Duncanson, with an effort to appear unconscious.

"N-n-no! perhaps not."

"Miss M'Killop looked very queer, I thought."

"Ah?"

"Very; what were you two fighting about on the cliff? I saw you."

"Fighting on the cliff!" replied the factor, quite taken aback; "I—I—when?"

"You know when; and, by the by, it must

have been rather a serious row, for you never looked near her afterwards. All the way down, in the yacht, you were monopolising her, but coming back you seemed to throw up the cards and resign the game to the adversary. You don't suppose I haven't noticed the game? but I hope you are not really going to let yourself be beat by a fellow like that!"

"You jump very quickly to your conclusions, Duncanson," said Tainsh, "and I will make so bold as to follow your lead. Surely *you* don't suppose that I haven't noticed another little game? and also that somebody who monopolised somebody all the way to Aberlorna, never went near somebody all the way home? What could be the meaning of that? The adversary, as you call him, is perhaps attractive in more quarters than one. I can see as far into a millstone as most people, and I will repeat to you what you have said to me, 'I hope you are not going to let yourself be beat by a fellow like that.'"

Tainsh's shot, fired in self-defence, but little more than at random, hit the target in the centre of the bull's-eye, and roused into activity what had been but a slumbering or unacknowledged suspicion; and Duncanson so far lost his self-control, that he jumped up and exclaimed in great excitement, "You have nothing to go upon, have you, in saying that? I have noticed nothing — hardly even the slightest conversation—between Morna and this infernal Cameron; have you? He seemed to be all on the other tack—trying to cut you out—what do you mean?"

"Well, I only use my eyes and my ears. Mrs M'Killop told me that, before Miss M'Killop came, Cameron was devoted to Morna, and they were always together. Now, though he may have transferred his affections to the other young lady, that is not to say that she has been so fickle. I've noticed something in her manner to him, too, that—but, after all, it is only a surmise, and I hope you have good reason to know that it is groundless?"

"No, I haven't, confound her and him and the whole crew! I've done with them. She may marry him, and be hanged; and he may marry them both: I wish he would, and get transported for bigamy."

"Ah!" said the lawyer, who had thus entirely succeeded in turning the tables, "I see I was right; I thought it was a row, and a serious one, too; but you are right not to let yourself be played fast and loose with—to be used as a cat's-paw—nothing could be more humiliating; and I fancy that's about the line you were taking with her to-day.—asserting yourself, I fancy? I'm a pretty shrewd hand at a guess, you see."

"Well," said Duncanson, "I can't say you're altogether wrong. I took deuced good care to let her know that I wasn't to be trifled with; and she must be vainer than I think, if she hopes to get any more attention from me. I never make up a quarrel, you know; it's against my rules. After all, it's as well I lost my temper; I might have got into a scrape—proposed, and got engaged, or something of that sort—which would have been a bad business for me. A fellow sometimes gets carried farther than he means, and they jump at you — Lord bless you! they jump at you, and you are booked before you can say 'knife.' I'm well out of it. She may whistle for me now. The cheek of the thing, though, is really too good! The idea of Cameron being set up as *my* rival! ha! ha! ha!" Something in the sound of his laughter, however, belied the speaker's *insouciant* tone almost as much as the short energetic sentence which followed after a pause. "I hate that fellow worse than poison—I would ruin him if I could."

"I have no love for him myself," said Tainsh; "I can't stand a man with his airs."

"I wish we could do something to floor him."

"Leave him to himself — give him rope enough, and he'll do the trick without any help from us. If he takes a step which I think he will take, I know of something that might get him into a rare mess. I may tell you of it at another time, but not now; it would be premature in the mean time."

"Out with it, Tainsh; I'm as close as wax."

"No, no; it would compromise others unnecessarily. You must wait."

"Pass the brandy, and we'll drink to his grief."

The two worthies were in this pious act, when the door opened and Bertrand stalked into the room with more than ordinary loftiness of demeanour. Had he been in the mood to observe, he might well have noticed the flurried looks of the two men, and been surprised at the nervous *empressement* with which Tainsh welcomed him and invited him to join in their potations.

"I am not here for pleasure, Mr Tainsh," he replied; "I have something of importance to say to you personally, if Mr Duncanson will have the goodness to retire."

"This is not the time or the place for business; and I'm not going to be sent to bed to suit your convenience," said Duncanson.

"Oh, Mr Cameron," said Tainsh, "there can be no hurry about anything between you and me; and, for the matter of that, no reason that I can see why it should not be said before Mr Duncanson."

"As you please, then," said Bertrand, "so be it. Well, Mr Tainsh, my business, in a word, is to demand an apology of the most ample kind, for your outrageously insolent conduct to Miss M'Killop, to-day."

"Sir!— Miss M'Killop?— to-day?" stammered Tainsh, utterly staggered by this direct and unexpected charge; "I don't understand."

"Your memory must be very short, if you don't; have the goodness to collect yourself, and make the required apology at once."

"And pray, sir, by what authority do you come to me with such a demand?"

"I come on my own authority?"

"And you expect me to obey it."

"Most certainly I shall take good care that you do."

"Oh, you will! as how?"

"The methods and alternatives are perfectly simple."

"I suppose you mean 'calling out'?"

"Well, although I might lose caste a little, still, considering the circumstances, and that your local position gives you the *entrée* to gentlemen's society on terms of equality, I would certainly call you out."

"Ha! ha!" laughed Tainsh; "duelling is a capital crime; you must have a small opinion of my wits if you think that I, a respectable, established man of business, am likely to run myself into a hole like that, to suit the humour of a hectoring young officer, who has nothing to lose."

"You would not go out, then?"

"Certainly not; and what next?"

"The next course is very unpleasant, but it is inevitable. I shall have to horsewhip you."

Bertrand said this with a decided composure, that left no doubt as to the fulfilment of the intention. Now Tainsh was no coward, and he was a sturdy fellow, to whom such a threat, from a physical point of view, need have had no particular terrors; but Tainsh was a lawyer, a factor, a man of business, and the idea of his being engaged in a midnight brawl, in a client's house, with a client's friend, which would be bruited over the whole district—for publicity would, of course, be Bertrand's object—was not to be entertained for an instant. His reputation would be shaken, his business would be damaged, and last, if not least, the story of his rejection would necessarily become public. Rapidly reviewing these considerations, he looked at Bertrand for an instant without replying, and seeing in his face no indication that he would not be as good as his word, he changed his tactics accordingly, and replied, "These are foolish words, Mr Cameron—very; the idea of a duel is preposterous: and if you ventured to take the other step (though what you suppose me to be made of I don't know), it would only bring yourself into trouble. It would be my duty to proceed against you legally for the assault; although, of course, I should have to act at the moment in self-defence, and probably with adequate vigour. How your military position would be affected by a scandal of the sort, you best know; how it would affect your position with your uncle, no one knows better than I do. So it is best to take a reasonable view of the matter; and if I have said anything in a moment of heat to displease Miss M'Killop, I shall be happy to apologise for it to her proper representative; but I can't conceive on what principle I am to look on you in that light."

"The simplest of all principles: Miss M'Killop is my betrothed; it concerns me, therefore, more than any one else, to protect her from insult."

"Betrothed, Mr Cameron!"

"I have said so; I trust you have no objection."

"Oh dear no! I'm surprised, of course."

"And why, sir? That I was preferred to you? does *that* surprise you?"

"You are introducing an irrelevant supposition" (with a hasty glance at Duncanson). "I was only surprised at the rapid transfer of your affections; but these are go-ahead days."

"I am ignorant of what you allude to."

"One has heard stories, you see, of attentions to another lady—only a week or two ago—marked attentions, constant companionship—private interviews—romantic walks, and all the duetting and flirting that make up a courtship according to common folks' minds; but then there is so much gossip going about, one never knows what to believe."

"On my authority," said Bertrand, suddenly recalling the rallyings of Pigott, and (somewhat innocently) startled and indignant to find that others had, in serious earnest, put the same construction on his free intercourse with Morna—"on my authority, you may assure your friends, the gossips, that no transfer of affections has taken place; and, let me add, that it is most unseemly and ungentlemanlike to introduce another lady's name into a discussion which in no way concerns her."

"You asked me why I was surprised, and I have answered you honestly," said Tainsh, sulkily. "We don't understand the habits of professional heart-breakers in these parts; but, of course, it must be part of their system to produce as strong an effect on the victim, to get as much amusement out of the conquest as possible, and still, at the end, to be able to assure the next subject that she is not merely being favoured with a transfer. The feelings of the last victim" (with another glance at Duncanson) "are of course immaterial, except as affording a certificate of success to the lady-killer."

"I see you wish to have another quarrel, on an independent subject, Mr Tainsh, and you shall have your wish; but one thing at a time, if you please."

"I have, and I desire, no quarrel with you; but I have a right to my thoughts."

"To your thoughts, yes; but not to express them when they are insulting. Enough of this, though; will you give me the desired apology?"

"I can have no objection to repeat what I honestly feel."

"You will have the goodness, then, to put it in writing, and give it to me in the morning. But remember, it must be ample; I will have no shuffling." And with this Bertrand left the room.

Tainsh and Duncanson looked at each other in silence till the last echoes of his footsteps on the stairs died away, and then Tainsh said, "There's an Emperor for you! His Majesty the King of Hearts!"

"I don't understand all these allusions, Tainsh," said Duncanson. "I don't want to pry into your affairs, although I'll not pretend that I don't see how matters stand with you and Miss M'Killop; but what is the real truth about the other affair? what is this about the other girl that made him so angry?"

"Well, Duncanson, I don't want to pry into your affairs, but I think I see pretty well how matters stand with you. In fact, honestly, we've both been cut out by this fellow."

"He is engaged to *your* young lady."

"And yours is over head and ears in love with him; any fool can see that. Propose to her—if you have not done it already—and I'll wager a hundred pounds to a brass farthing you are refused."

"And he knows it, you think?"

"Knows what?"

"That Morna cares for him."

"Knows it? bless you! I should rather

think he did. He's chuckling up-stairs now with that English snail; he's bragging to him, you may depend upon it, and telling him how these poor devils down-stairs are hanging their heads, and how he has bowled them both out in a fortnight."

Duncanson thundered out a tremendous oath. To be refused at all was bad enough, but to be refused by a girl because she loved another man, who had won her in a few days, only for amusement—only to brag about—and who had tired of her and cast her aside when his conquest was complete—and that man the man he hated of all others—was exasperation for any one indeed, but for this vain, domineering soul, the very gall of bitterness.

"What *can* be done to him?" cried Duncanson.

"You can call him out and shoot him; you're not professional."

"I have no pretext."

"I should have thought that picking a quarrel would have come easy to you."

"Yes, yes, that might be easy enough; but then, you see, a man only gets laughed at for fighting nowadays."

"You're prudent, like me, I see," said Tainsh, dryly.

"I don't funk, if you mean that."

"Oh no, I don't mean that, or I should imply that I funked myself, which I don't."

"Do you suppose he means to marry the girl?"

"Of course he does; he's really wild about her: I've seen that all along."

"If there was only some way of running through the marriage—of breaking his infernal heart! Do you suppose he has money enough to marry?"

"If his uncle chooses, and M'Killop chooses."

"Will they?"

"Who can tell? I do know a little something that would very soon set his uncle against it, but in my position, for many reasons, I couldn't use it."

"Tell it to me!" cried Duncanson, eagerly.

"No, no — better not; underhand games never pay."

"Tell me, Tainsh, and I'll work it on my own account."

"It would be traced to me."

"No fear; I'll swear secrecy."

And, after a good deal of wheedling and cajoling, Tainsh, being not so much as half-hearted in his resistance, was induced, at last, to communicate something to Duncanson, which sent that worthy to bed with the first gleam of consolation in his soul, since his hopes as a lover had received their overthrow that afternoon.

The morning post came in very early at Cairnarvoch ; and when the party assembled at breakfast on the following day, they found that Mr Tainsh and Mr Duncanson had started an hour before ; letters, by a strange coincidence, having called them both unexpectedly away.

A packet for Bertrand lay on the hall table, addressed in Mr Tainsh's hand ; and its contents were all that could be desired.

CHAPTER XVII.

BERTRAND's eventful day had come to a conclusion at last; and now, alone in his own room, he contemplated all that it had brought forth. The stormy episode with Mr Tainsh had closed, for the present, the period of storms; and a rapture of peace came upon his spirit, like "slumber's anodyne to fevered frames," or that calmest of all calms that lies so softly on the summer sea at dawn, when a tempest's ruffian winds have folded their dark wings, and hushed the faintest accent of all their myriad, sinister voices.

Deep and perfect peace was on his spirit; and, indeed, if there be a moment when that is possible to us mortals here below, it is then —surely it is then—when Love, that has come to the heart still fresh and pure with the dew of life's morning, catches the first low tremulous harmonies of Requital's voice,—those utterances sounding like some music astray from Paradise,—that never, never can be all forgotten, but will, and must, come back to us; ever plaintive because from the past, yet strangely clear for all the distance they may come, yet strangely sweet for all the passionate sadness they may express. Clear and sweet these echoes come, falling into the minor key, when, as they sweep over the dreary steppes of our ruined lives, they pass the graves of our fairest hopes, and reach us across the ashes of that First Love that gave them voice. Deep and perfect peace, therefore, was on Bertrand's spirit; for this was first love, this was true love—fully accepted, with every assurance of requital. It had struck Pigott, who knew him well, as strange that Cupid's torch had not been earlier applied to that exaltedly-imaginative spirit; and so it may appear to others who are less intimate with him; but, in truth, the very exaggeration of those qualities which might have been supposed to render him susceptible, had hitherto kept him heart-whole. It was no absorption in the pursuits and pleasures of his age and profession; it was no lack of opportunity; nor yet was it that his mind was averted from the subject, in that affected scepticism with which certain of our youth ape the tone of cynical models. On the contrary, the beauty, the poetry, the romance, so inextricably interwoven with the *belle passion*, had produced the profoundest impression on a mind extraordinarily impressionable by such influences. But the result was not that he recognised a goddess in every garrison Dulcinea, or erected a new altar, and called upon a new divinity, with every change of quarters. Deeply fastidious in all things, he had long ago evolved for himself an ideal, endowed with exquisite purity and refinement, warmed with all gracious womanly tenderness, quickened with bright intelligence, and wrapped in the bewitching mantle of that beauty in which his soul delighted. In the contemplation of this ideal—in this shadow-worship—he had been content to wait, till, clothed in reality, his ideal should descend from the realm of dreams and visions, and into his calm adoration breathe the warm breath of passion's ecstatic life. He had not surrendered his heart to the guidance of a succession of "summer pilots unto the shores of nothing." He had been content to wait, and he had waited, unswerving from his allegiance, true to his ideal. But now he told himself that she had come—his goddess—his very own; and, with the rapture of a devotee, he had laid his offering—the best a man can offer—his true, fresh heart, upon her altar. It was accepted, and he was at peace. Was she in very truth the realisation of his ideal? Were all these fair attributes hers indeed? No matter. No ideal *can* be realised; approximation is all that can be hoped for. Suffice it that Bertrand believed he had found what he had waited for; and, even supposing that he was congratulating himself and finding peace in a fool's paradise, perhaps in such matters that is better (since a paradise of some sort is essential) than no paradise at all.

And so his day finished, and the night was light about him; for, in the pageantry of his happy dreams, moved, amid myrtles and roses, one constant vision, in whose presence clouds and darkness were impossible.

We fear we may seem to have been guilty of a rather ungallant partiality in dwelling thus upon Bertrand's feelings, and postponing those of the fair being who inspired them.

But it is a more difficult and a more delicate task to deal with the subtler movements of the female heart; and, after all, "in love, if love be love, if love be ours," there must be a sufficiently strong resemblance between the male and female edition of the passion to excuse us from again traversing the ground we have got over, in speaking of Bertrand. Shall we therefore simply credit Eila with the same feelings we have ascribed to him, making due allowance for the difference of sex and temperament, and remembering that she is betrothed to him? Perhaps, on the whole, it will be better to let her speak for herself.

If there be a time when the heart, whether male or female, craves the sympathy of another heart, it is at such crisises when it is filled to overflowing with thoughts which the poet describes as too sweet for utterance, but which, in practice, are uttered with a freedom which often makes their sweetness not a little cloying to the confidential recipient. Even Bertrand had ventured his sweet tale to Pigott, undeterred by the uncongeniality of his friend; and it is not surprising that Eila should have seized an early opportunity of unbosoming herself to some one; and who more appropriate than her warm-hearted step-sister?

It was by no means a final "good-night," therefore, which she wished that young lady when they separated in the hall, on leaving the drawing-room; for, not many minutes after, arrayed in a bewitching dressing-gown, over which floated loose her beautiful wealth of hair, and wearing the air of a young lady who has come prepared for, and bent upon, a protracted session, she entered Morna's room.

Morna was in the hands of the tormentor— that is, she was having her hair brushed by an extremely acid maid (colleague of the spectral M'Kenzie), who contrived, when her temper was, as at present, and as it generally was, out of order, to make the process not a painless one. Morna was tired, out of spirits—shall we say even cross?—and the Abigail's operations were not at all acting sedatively, so it was scarcely in a tone of welcome that she greeted her visitor.

"Is that you, Eila?"

"Yes, dearest Morna, it is; I have come to have a little talk with you. Is that tiresome hair nearly done?"

"It will take ten minutes, at the least, to do it justice, after *this* day's work," snorted the maid, who felt all "pleasuring" to be a personal injury, and now saw an opportunity of avenging herself.

"Oh! never mind," cried Eila; "do send her away, Morna dear; it *is* so tiresome to be kept waiting, and I have so much to say; do send her away, and I'll brush it for you myself."

Morna did not seem to share her step-sister's impatience.

"It is so comfortable," she replied, "when one is tired; and surely what you have to say can keep for ten minutes."

The maid's exasperation on perceiving that there was something "particular" to be talked about after her departure—some joyous confidence, some possible fun and merriment—converted her unwittingly into Eila's ally; for she so tweaked and twisted her patient's hair that Morna fairly rebelled, ordering her peremptorily to desist and leave the room.

"Well, Eila?" she said, when the woman had gone—"well, Eila?" Her tone implied, "Please say what you have to say as quickly as possible, and then leave me."

Eila made no reply in words, but fixed her beautiful eyes for an instant on her step-sister, with a bright and meaning smile, then threw her arms round her neck, and covered her with kisses.

When this had gone on for a little, without any reasonable prospect of release, Morna disengaged herself firmly, and, as if in answer to a verbal communication, quietly remarked, "You refused him, I suppose?"

"Refused him, Morna? What? How? Do *you* know? Who could have——"

"No one has spoken to me about the matter; but of course Mr Tainsh proposed to you to-day?"

"Mr Tainsh?"

"Yes; did he not?"

"Oh! of course he did."

"Of course. I knew that; and you refused him?"

"Of course I did—the abominable, presumptuous creature!"

"Poor Mr Tainsh!"

"Not 'poor Mr Tainsh' at all; he has only got his desert."

"He could not have expected it, though;

it must have been a surprise to him—a painful one."

"Morna!"

"Eila!"

"You are cross and disagreeable, and I have a great mind to tell you no more."

"You must do exactly as you please."

"Well then, I will tell you."

"Very well; do."

"There was more than one proposal to-day."

"Ah! you know that?"

"Yes, indeed—but only one refusal;" and again Eila flung her arms round Morna's neck.

"Stop, stop!" cried the latter. "You are all wrong—you are mistaken—I *did* refuse him."

"What?" cried Eila, uncoiling herself with a start.

"I refused him."

"Refused *whom?*"

"Mr Duncanson, of course."

"Oh, indeed!" cried Eila—"oh, indeed! I wasn't thinking of—of him" ("or you," she might have added). "And you refused him? Very imprudent, was it not? I should say *very* imprudent; but that is not what I was going to speak about;—fancy what a curious coincidence! two proposals in one day! That makes four altogether, and I am only nineteen! but this is the last, for I have taken him. I am engaged, Morna—engaged to Bertrand Cameron."

One would say that the announcement need not have occasioned great *surprise* to Morna; and indeed, if it did, she concealed the emotion pretty successfully. A flush, a slight quiver, and the sudden tightening of her hand upon a book she held—these were the few external signs that Eila's words conveyed to her intelligence that strongly affected her, and in an instant she replied gravely, but kindly, as she kissed her step-sister—

"I congratulate you, dear Eila. I hope you will be very, very happy—I think you ought to be."

"I think so, dearest; yes, indeed, I am sure of it: for you know he *is* charming—and the silly creature is *so* devoted to me; quite absurd and childish, in fact; and — and I — well, I suppose I *do* like him a good deal—although, of course, I have only told him that I like him a *little*; and if papa does not object, I think we ought to be very happy indeed. I must tell you all about it, though, and how it came about. You see, Mr Tainsh, &c. &c. &c."

But we know all about it already, so we shall let the conversation go on unreported till the point where Eila, having exhausted all her confidences, and said all that is usually said in such interviews, about herself and her lover, felt inclined to satisfy her curiosity and her interest in Morna's affairs, by reverting to what had been said about Mr Duncanson.

"Now, Morna," she said, "after all these confessions, you must give me some in return. You refused him, you said—and I think it was very imprudent. Of course it was only a temporary refusal, and the temptation to snub him would of course be great; but you know his temper is so very high. It was not wise to risk it. I really don't know but what you may have a great deal of trouble to get him back. It will be a difficult matter I am sure" (Eila spoke with all the earnestness of an enthusiastic expert in the art of man-taming); " but I'll tell you what you ought to do, Morna dear; you ought to go straight to your mother —she will not be in bed yet—tell her the *whole truth,* and make her send a note to Mr Duncanson the *first thing* in the morning, asking him to speak to her before he goes, or the chances are he will be off before daylight, and then you may *never* get him back again."

"An excellent plan, Eila, if I wanted to get him back; but you see, as it happens, I do *not.*"

"I'm sure I don't know what you can be waiting for, then, Morna. Here is ten thousand—fifteen thousand—perhaps twenty thousand a-year; is that not enough? Of course a poor soldier is good enough for a humble person like me, and I am thankful that I am not so hard to please; but I suppose nothing under a duke would be good enough for the descendant of all the M'Whannels and M'Cuaigs."

"Don't be cross, Eila dear; you are very kind to take such an interest in my affairs; but I assure you I have no such high notions. I simply refused Mr Duncanson because I don't like him; besides, as I have often told you, I have quite resolved never to marry."

"Never to marry! my dear girl, this is the first time I ever heard of it; and this is about the last occasion on which you could except me to believe in, or sympathise with, any such nonsense. Ah, Morna! if you knew, if you only knew, what it is to love!"

"Well, Eila, I think even you will admit that Mr Duncanson is scarcely the person to teach me; but I daresay it is very true what you say, that love would make a great difference in one's views of matrimony; but you see it does not fall to the lot of every one; and I must end off where I began, by saying that I hope you will be as happy as you ought to be, when the course of true love runs so smooth; —and now I think we had better say 'Good night.'"

And so Morna brought the conversation to a close, kissing and dismissing her step-sister; and before she went to bed she wrote a letter to her aunts, now staying in Scotland, and at no great distance from Cairnarvoch, but about to return to their home in the south of England, begging to be allowed to join them at once, although the customary period of her residence with her mother had still a month to run.

CHAPTER XVIII.

THE breakfast-table at Cairnarvoch, on the morning after all these exciting events, was unusually quiet. The only two members of the party not thoroughly preoccupied were Pigott and M'Killop, neither of whom contributed much, as a rule, to the conversation; and, this morning, they had it all to themselves, an opportunity which they "improved" by a frugal use of monosyllables.

One result, however, was satisfactory to all parties—that the meal was soon over.

Poor Mrs M'Killop was in a terrible state of mystification;—she feared much, she suspected much, but she was certain of nothing. The night before, she had confidently expected a communication from her daughter or her stepdaughter—perhaps from both—but she had been disappointed; and as it concerned her dignity not to initiate the subjects which gnawed her heart with anxious curiosity, by a superhuman effort of self-denial, she had refrained from extorting by question, the confidence she had expected to be spontaneous. But this could not last for ever; and this morning she said to herself, " If *they* don't speak at once, *I* must; it is my solemn duty as a parent;" in pursuance of which determination she signalled the young ladies, as they left the breakfast-room, to come to her boudoir. Neither of them, however, thought fit to understand the signal—Morna rapidly making her escape in another direction, and Eila sauntering carelessly out of the hall-door on to the terrace, where she was immediately joined by Bertrand.

"I wish to speak to you, Eila," cried her step-dame from the doorway.

"I shall be with you immediately, dear mamma," was the reply; "only let me have five minutes of this delightful morning sun on the terrace first."

It is not difficult to conceive what, under such circumstances, " five minutes of the delightful morning sun upon the terrace " became. Very rapidly the terrace itself was abandoned for a retreat more appropriate to the interview,—where, among thick, shadowy foliage, the morning sun could only contribute in a very minor degree to the delight of the occasion, and where, indeed, the noontide sun, suddenly blazing through the branches overhead, found the lovers with the five minutes still unexhausted. But Eila might have been pardoned for her want of punctuality by the strictest martinet; on such occasions it is, if it ever is, excusable; for where a conversation has a tendency to go round and round in a circle of iteration, the progress of the dialogue to any special conclusion, however fast the words may flow, can neither be marked nor rapid. Far be it from us to follow that dialogue in its details. It certainly would not read well. Accompanied by illustrative diagrams, it might be more amusing; but as it is, it is better left to the imagination. Bertrand would inevitably bore us with his imagery and his raptures, for a very little of that sort of thing goes a very long way, when one is not personally alluded to. "And always, always you will love me—me only—and always thus?" the sweetest temper would give way under a score of repetitions of this, and similar questions, so we shall be as general as possible. For all that is said to the contrary about women, perhaps their views on such occasions are, as a matter of fact, more practical than those of men.

To a certain extent, the pleasurable excitement of the affair has been on their side all along; they have had observances, homage, worship, and only such an infinitesimal amount of uncertainty as to season what might otherwise have become insipid; and therefore, when the proposal is made, the sport of the thing is over, and its business aspect begins at once to present itself. The male being, on the other hand, only begins to have his innings when his suit is accepted. It is only natural that he should like to have his little share of antenuptial worship; that he should like to be told in words, what maidenly reserve should not (theoretically) have allowed even a look hitherto to reveal; that he should like to expatiate a little, in the blissful regions of romance—just a very little—before betaking himself to the prose of figures and dates, and the fateful tribunal of earthy parents. Eila justified our theory on this occasion; and, though satisfactorily reciprocating her lover's protestations, endeavoured, every now and then, to insinuate between his raptures, the thin edge of the practical consideration. As, for example, thus: "We shall be horribly poor, shan't we, dear Bertrand?"

"Horribly, I suppose. I don't know, though —I have four hundred a-year; my uncle might double it, I should think. He certainly ought to, for he says I want steadying; and if anything *can* steady a man, of course, marriage must. Oh, we shall be all right somehow. Married to such an angel, such an &c. &c."

"We shall have prospects, though, shan't we, dearest?" insinuates the practical angel.

"Oh yes; we shall get Aberlorna, I suppose, if my uncle doesn't marry—and he won't, especially when he sees what an angel, what an &c. &c." (Diagram.)

"You must speak to papa at once, Bertrand; you had better come and do it now."

"Oh, there's no hurry; I'll make it all right with him, presently."

"But it ought to be done at once; it ought to have been done before we came out here. I can't bear concealments—they are so wrong; and we have no right to be so happy till we have his consent."

"You dear, delightful, dutiful little angel! but let us have five minutes more—only five minutes—and then I promise to go to him. Will he be difficult to manage?"

"It is impossible to say: he is devoted to me, but then who could resist *you?*" (Diagram.)

After a great many renewals, Bertrand's five minutes' lease of beatitude was at last brought finally to a close, and he suffered himself to be led back to the house to have his *mauvais quart d'heure* with Mr M'Killop. Once in that gentleman's presence, he did not waste much time in preliminary flourishes, or in those ghastly attempts to lead neatly up to the subject, as usual on such occasions, as they are invariably abortive. Being frank and ardent, he plunged into the business at once.

"Can I speak to you for half a minute, Mr M'Killop?"

"Certainly."

"Thanks; I've just come to say—I daresay you'll be awfully surprised, and perhaps angry, but it can't be helped—I've just come to say that I hope you'll allow me to marry your daughter Eila, for I never loved any one before, and I'll never love any one again, as I love her; and I've told her so; and she——and it's all right."

Mr M'Killop rose hastily from his chair; he was, as we all know, singularly taciturn and apparently phlegmatic; but he rose hastily from his chair, and his face flushed, and his eyes brightened, and, for an instant, he allowed himself to betray that Bertrand's abrupt communication had powerfully moved him in some way or another: for an instant, too, it seemed that he was going to express himself with corresponding animation; but that impulse was checked, and, recovering himself, he said quietly, and with a half-smile, "By 'all right,' you mean that my daughter reciprocates your feelings?"

"Yes," said Bertrand, "she has accepted me; and we only want your consent to be perfectly happy: you won't refuse it, I hope?"

"My dear young friend," said M'Killop, resuming his seat and speaking with averted eyes, "the question you put is a very grave question. Young hearts leap to their conclusions, but grey heads reach them slowly and carefully—slowly, my dear young friend, *and* carefully."

"But, after all," said Bertrand, "it doesn't require much reflection. Here are two people determined to marry each other, and no one else; they're both eligible for each other, and—and what more has to be said?"

"That is—excuse me for saying so—a very superficial view of the matter. There are many considerations to be taken into account when marriage is the question. Personally, no sort of objection to you could be brought by the most fastidious. I like you—I like you much. You are a fine young fellow, Mr Cameron; any girl might be proud of your attachment, and so, I make no doubt, is my daughter; but there is the old story—the sordid part of the business. We can't live on love, and we can't marry without the prospect of something more substantial than love—you must see that yourself."

"Of course, of course; but that would be all right somehow."

"'Somehow' is a bad source of income for a young couple to begin life on, Mr Cameron," said M'Killop, with a good-humoured laugh.

"Yes, but I am sure it could be contrived—enough could be got together."

M'Killop did not reply at once, but rose and walked up and down the room, apparently plunged in profound meditation, Bertrand watching his face with the anxiety of one who strives to read his fate. At last Mr M'Killop stopped, and asked—

"Would your uncle approve of this marriage, do you think?"

"Approve of it? of course he would. He is always saying that he wishes to see me 'steadier' and 'more settled;' and I suppose every one will admit that marriage is the direct road to all that sort of thing."

"He is a proud man, I believe."

"I daresay he is—and will be prouder still when his nephew is married to the most perfect woman in the world."

"Ha! ha!" laughed M'Killop; "you must first of all get him to look at her through your spectacles." Then, after relapsing into his abstraction for a little, he continued: "The property is at his own disposal, I think?"

VOL. II.   L

"Well, yes — that is, with conditions. I believe it is not exactly entailed, but destined, or settled, or something, on me, if he has no children, and I do nothing very diabolical—nothing that he disapproves of."

"And you don't think Sir Roland would consider this marriage very diabolical?" laughed M'Killop.

"My dear sir, can you doubt that he will be enchanted? He is a cold man, but I am sure that, at heart, he is really kind. Then he will simply adore Eila—every one must; and there is no saying how generous he may be!" cried Bertrand, led away, for the moment, by his special pleading, but salving his conscience at once by adding, "Provided he is pleased, which is a matter of course."

Again M'Killop paced the room in deep thought, betraying now and then, in his appearance, symptoms of the agitation which had marked the opening of their interview.

"What on earth can the man be thinking about? The thing is as simple as the alphabet. He's not against it, however — that's clear," thought Bertrand.

After some time M'Killop spoke again.

"I can only repeat, my dear young friend, what I have said before, that I like you much personally, and that I do not conceal from myself that such a marriage would have many advantages for my daughter; but — but — there is always a 'but,' Mr Cameron, in these things — there are considerations that must be considered, and calculations that must be made; and on the whole, perhaps, if you would let me think the matter over for an hour or so, I should be able to discuss it with you more satisfactorily."

Hereupon Bertrand withdrew, and remained alone, and in feverish excitement, till, in about the time named, a servant announced that Mr M'Killop would be glad to see him in his business-room. Betrand found his host much more alive and awake than usual, with an unclouded brow, and a manner that was for him quite gay and lively. "Well, Mr Cameron," he said, "I have been thinking over our little difficulty, and, I assure you, with hearty goodwill; and I hope, by making some sacrifice — which I shall be glad to make, mind you — that I can put matters in a satisfactory train."

"You are far too kind and good!" cried Bertrand.

"Wait, wait. First of all I make it a positive condition that you get your uncle's consent. I could not hear of the marriage without that. Apart altogether from money considerations, I could not allow it. We may or may not be people of extraction, but we have our feelings of self-respect. You understand me, I am sure?"

"Certainly, sir; and I know what an excellent right you have to respect yourself!" cried Bertrand, with pardonable enthusiasm.

"Very well; Sir Roland's consent must precede the marriage, and something more; but, first of all, let me tell you what I propose to do for you, pecuniarily, myself. I have the reputation of being rich, and I do not pretend that it is unfounded; but one portion of my fortune is embarked in trade, subject to its vicissitudes and uncertainties. The other half is now being invested in land in Scotland; and that, as you are aware, impairs the income of a capital hitherto invested in carefully-selected securities, paying a high rate of interest. Ahem?"

"Yes," said Bertrand, not quite knowing what was expected of him.

"Very good; my present income will thus be reduced, and the land to be invested in is, and always has been, intended to pass, after me, to my son—a deserving son, sir, who has never given me a moment's anxiety, and whom I shall feel it my duty to assist otherwise to the utmost of my power, so that his position after me, as a landowner, may be as good a one as he is entitled to expect. Ahem?"

"Clearly," said Bertrand, not quite seeing, however, how these noble views for the son tended to the provision of the daughter.

"Very well; let us say that, independent of the land, my capital, subject to risks as above, might realise a hundred and fifty thousand pounds at the least."

"An immense sum!" cried Bertrand.

"Very well; one-third of this—subject as above—shall be my daughter's after my decease, if she marries you; on the condition that Sir Roland sanctions the marriage, and settles the reversion of Aberlorna irrevocably on you and your heirs. Ahem?"

"You are far too generous, Mr M'Killop."

"Listen; I will also undertake during my lifetime to add an annual equivalent to any sum he may annually allow you, subject to the above conditions."

"I never dreamt of such munificence!" cried Bertrand; "and pray believe me that I had no thought of fortune, or even that Eila would have any money at all, when I proposed to her: you are really too generous."

"Well, Mr Cameron, I daresay you can understand that I have a partiality for my daughter; and I don't really see that I could make a better use of my money;—do you? ha! ha! But, to return to the practical, we must, first of all, get Sir Roland's consent; and meantime we must exercise a little patience. The time will pass quickly enough. You had better write to your uncle at once; offer my respects, and say that, after mature and anxious consideration, I have given my provisional sanction, and that I am prepared to do so-and-so, subject to so-and-so, as stated before; and that we await his reply—anxiously. You incline to think he will consent?"

"I haven't a doubt of it; your munificence would alone be sufficient to secure that."

"That is good; I sincerely hope so; and now go away and be happy with Eila."

So Bertrand went away, treading upon air. Probably M'Killop had talked more in the last hour than he had done altogether since the beginning of the shooting season; and Bertrand was satisfied that, in all his previous life, he had never talked to better purpose. Nothing could well be more satisfactory and agreeable. Fortune seemed to be literally pelting Bertrand with her favours. His rival distanced, his lady-love won, and, on the top of it all, a practical parent blessing him with the unction of the old stage-uncle, and hurling golden promises of fortune at him with dramatic generosity!

The course of true love was running smooth, deep, and rapid, the sound of wedding-bells mingling with its soothing song—surely gliding to some peaceful summer sea? surely never to mingle with tempestuous billows, and lose its sweet life in a wilderness of storms?

While matters had been progressing thus happily in the business-room, Mrs M'Killop, smarting with a considerable sense of wrong, and with her curiosity piqued to the uttermost, had vainly waited all the morning for Eila, and as vainly searched for her own daughter. We know how Eila had been occupied. As for Morna, she had felt herself by no means in the humour for the maternal cross-examination. She knew that what she had to announce would occasion to her mother both anger and disappointment; and never, in all her life, had she felt less able to bear the coarse outbreaks of that lady's sometimes violent temper. To be put to the question as to minute facts; to have her motives ruthlessly probed; to have all the delicate workings of her heart—many of them not consciously admitted by herself—paraded and reviewed by so unsympathetic an agency, would have been, just then, intolerable to her. The very vitality of her mother's manner was terribly antipathetic to her present feelings. So she had avoided her, and gone away out among the silent woods, instinctively seeking from Nature, who never yet deceived the heart that loved her, that tender, placid sympathy which her heart craved. Mrs M'Killop meantime had waited and sought in vain; and the mystery that shrouded the proceedings of yesterday became more mysterious as she felt that the two young ladies were avoiding her for a purpose; so that she met them at luncheon, bristling with curiosity and wrath. During that meal she conducted herself with silent dignity, and, at its conclusion, remarked to the two culprits—" Morna, I desire that you will come with me to the boudoir; as for you, Eila, I will not trouble you to break another engagement with me."

" Dear mamma, I'll come at once!" cried Eila.

" You are very good, I'm sure, but I could not think of troubling you; and, for the present, I am engaged with my own daughter, if I can hope that she will condescend so far."

Mrs M'Killop was evidently in the most abominable of tempers; so neither young lady made any further controversy; Eila going away by herself, and Morna following her mother to the inevitable interview.

" I think," began Mrs M'Killop, as soon as they were seated in the chamber of inquisition —" I think, Morna, I have a right to feel that you are treating me ill."

" I am sure, mamma, I would never do so willingly," was the reply.

"You have avoided me ever since our return from the picnic. I am not blind, child; I know that something which you are anxious to conceal from me happened yesterday."

"No, indeed, mamma; I have nothing to conceal from you; but somehow I did not feel able last night, or even this morning, to tell you of what happened yesterday."

"I was right, then; something did happen?"

"Yes, mamma."

"Please go on, then; I detest all this sentimental mystery and fuss."

"I wish to make no fuss about it, but——"

"I declare you would try the temper of a saint: did James Duncanson propose to you?"

"Yes; I am sorry to say he did."

"Sorry!"

"Sincerely."

"Why?"

"Because I was compelled to do what may have pained him a little; and what, I fear, will disappoint you."

"Do you mean to tell me that you actually ventured to refuse him?"

Mrs M'Killop was of course morally certain that she had; but the question was dramatically necessary to justify surprise, which always runs so well with indignation.

"I did refuse him, mamma, and my principal regret in doing so was that I felt it would vex you; but I really couldn't help it."

"Oh! you couldn't help it, couldn't you?" sneered her mother, in a white heat.

"No, mamma, I could not."

"I presume, then, you have other secrets from me; perhaps you are engaged to some *partee* worthier of you—a duke, or a prince, or" (which was probably Mrs M'Killop's highest idea of distinction) "a nobleman in disguise?"

"No, mother, there is nothing of that sort in the way."

"Then, in the name of wonder, girl, what is it?"

"Nothing," said Morna, in a sad and weary tone.

"Nothing! you had best go to a nunnery, or a poor's-house, or the infirmary at once," snarled her mother. "I've had trouble enough with you and your up-bringing; I've given you the chance of an establishment, and you throw it away for some crotchet, as if it was— as if it was ditch-water. Fifteen thousand a-year! and a fine young man! And you—what are you but a pauper, or next thing to it? A position like what we used to have long ago! Thousands of acres! Part of the old M'Cuaig property too! Oh! you ungrateful — undutiful—artful—obstinate; and Eila——"

But this last consideration was too poignant; and here the angry mother burst into a torrent of tears, accompanied by gusts of maledictory sobbing, and spasmodic invocations of unutterable ancestors to rise from their tombs and testify against their worthless descendant. Morna bore it all with silent fortitude, and when the tempest had lulled a little, said—

"It grieves me sincerely, mamma, to vex you so; but our views about marriage are evidently altogether different, and we need not argue about it. I would do anything I possibly could to please you, but this I really could not—could *not* do."

"Go away out of my sight, you sly hypocrite!" roared the matron, with renewed vigour. "I hope the deluded young man will not give you another chance, when you come to your senses. You're—you're—not fit to be a good man's wife. I don't doubt but you've got some low, beggarly attachment—that's the secret of it. Well, go away and be married to any of the ghillies you please, or perhaps you would prefer a shepherd, or the postman, or— well, I've done with you."

"You have no right to speak so to me, mother," said Morna, roused to anger at last. "If 'the deluded young man,' as you call him, ever ventures to mention the subject to me again, I shall let him know my real reason for refusing him—that I loathe and despise him. I don't know how you dare to say that I am unfit to be a good man's wife. I never wish to be, and never shall be, any man's wife— good or bad; but I will not stay here to be so cruelly treated and spoken to, even by you, mother. I have already offered to go to my aunts before the time, and to-morrow I shall go to them. When you come to *your* senses, I may come back to you." Morna marched to the door, tragic and indignant, but, turning there, looked back at her mother, whose wrath, half paralysed by astonishment and a rising fear of having gone too far, was now oozing away in quiet tears.

Morna looked at her mother for a moment or two without speaking, then came back to her side, and said, "Mother, forgive me; I was wrong—we were both wrong. You were angry and did not know what you said; and I—oh! if you only knew how sad my heart is, and how really it grieves me to vex you, you would not drive me away with such words. I am sure you might believe that I would do anything that it was possible for me to do to please you; but this was not possible—it really was not."

Mrs M'Killop was somewhat impressed with Morna's speech, and replied in querulous but no longer insulting tones, "Yes, yes; that is always the way with young people nowadays. Ask them to do anything but what you particularly wish them to do, and what it is their duty to do, and they will obey you cheerfully."

"Well, mamma, I am quite certain that, with my feelings, it could not be my duty to do this; but it can do no good to argue about it." And hereupon Morna, seizing a moment of comparative peace to bring the interview to a close, kissed her mother and left the room. Before the perturbation of Mrs M'Killop's spirit had altogether calmed down, a gentle tap came to her door, and before she could either refuse or grant admittance, there entered to her, with graceful undulating motions, and a bright, but withal deprecating, smile on her lovely face — Eila. No visitor could have been more unwelcome at the moment. Mrs M'Killop's aversion to Eila, at all times sincere, was at this moment intensified by her daughter's refusal to play the only card which Eila appeared unable to trump; and, besides this, she was certain that Eila now came to announce to her the collapse of her own scheme, which would have removed that young lady from a trumping position for the future. Poor Mrs M'Killop! it was very hard upon her, to be sure, that her natural ally and her natural foe—in her mind, natural antagonists to each other—should both seem perversely determined to sacrifice even their own interests (as she read it) for the sake of thwarting her; that both strings to her bow should snap, both barrels miss fire. If either had been successful, the failure of the other would not have been so grievous. If Eila had "gone off," the ground would have been clear for Morna, for the future; and if Morna had accepted Mr

Duncanson, that would have consoled her mother for the continued misfortune of Eila's society. But both had failed, and the detestable *status quo* was all before her again. It was well, perhaps, that so much of her wrath had already found such free vent, or she might have been unable to exercise even a semblance of the control over herself which hitherto she had achieved, even in her keenest passages with the enemy. As it was, she rose from her seat with an angry flounce, and, though her manner was meant to express calm dignity, it was the intermittent flustery dignity of the turkey-cock. In this way she intimated that, as Eila had found it inconvenient to come to *her* in the morning, *she* now found it inconvenient to receive her, and begged to be left alone. If Morna's tale had been a different one, she could have afforded to listen with patience—perhaps even with interest—to the details of Mr Tainsh's discomfiture; but, as it was, she had no patience for anything that her step-daughter could say. Eila, altogether ignoring the *congé*, and the stormy symptoms which accompanied it, continued to advance upon her step-mother with smiles of archest significance, and—like a regiment reserving its fire till at close quarters—spoke not a word till she threw her arms round the astonished matron's neck, and kissed her ardently.

"Eila! Miss M'Killop! wh—what is the meaning of this—this exhibition?" gasped the step-dame, attempting to extricate herself from Eila's arms, who, however, only varied the caress by burying her head in her victim's ample bosom, with a sort of "rock-me-to-sleep-mother" *pose*, delightfully in contrast with the elder lady's attitude and expression. "I desire you — madam — I cannot — I will not——" gasped Mrs M'Killop, morally, if not physically, suffocated by the demonstration.

"Dearest mamma," murmured Eila, withdrawing a little—"dearest mamma, I am so, *so* happy!"

"What!" shouted the dame, plunging back so violently as to be in danger of turning a back somersault over the sofa behind her.

"So happy, so exquisitely happy!"

"And fine cause you have for it, no doubt!" snorted Mrs M'Killop.

"Yes, indeed, dear mamma; and *he* is quite pleased."

"Oh! *he* is quite pleased, is he? that is delightful. If *he* knew you as well as I do, *he* might well be pleased."

"Thanks! thanks! you" (closing) "dear, good, kind" (kiss), "flattering mamma."

"I pro-test I won't stand this impertinence any longer!" cried Mrs M'Killop, disengaging herself, and staring fiercely at Eila, who regarded her with meek astonishment. "Are you mad, Miss M'Killop?"

"If I am, it is only with too much happiness; but what *is* the matter with you?"

"The matter with me! the matter! the matter? Is this a seemly spirit to be in after what has occurred?"

"Why not?"

"Oh! to be sure, 'why not?' miss. This is the modern school, I suppose; this is 'the period'—this is quite correct, nowadays, of course. I'm an antediloovyan, I know. I had better go to the museums at once—among the ichsoruses, and the mammals, and the camels, or——"

"What *can* you mean, mamma?" cried Eila, with the widest eyes.

"All I can say is, if your father approves of

it, I don't: if you are to make game of his friends, I don't. I am a plain woman, but I am a lady by birth, and this is not our way, and I don't. My grandmother——"

"Mamma, what *are* you talking of?" and indeed the question was not uncalled for.

"If you choose to refuse a decent man's honourable proposals—to throw away chances you'll never get again, that's *your* affair; but you shan't come to giggle and triumph like—like—a mulatto, over him, to *me*, in *my* room; and so I tell you, miss. Perhaps it may amuse your maid—you can try her; it disgusts *me*, and so I tell you: and this is my *boo*door, and that is *the* door, and so I tell you."

"Dear mamma, I wasn't triumphing over a refusal—it is just the opposite. I was going to tell you of my engagement."

"Your engagement!" sneered Mrs M'Killop, with lofty incredulity. "Now, with my antediloovyan notions, do you know I actually supposed you had refused Mr Tainsh—I'm really quite behind the age."

"Not at all; I *did* refuse him."

"Oh! you did?—I see—and you've repented, and called him back; of course, with your over*whelming* charms, you have no doubt he will come; but some men have their foolish pride, and, do you know, I think it would be more delicate, to say the least of it, if you didn't give out your engagement to Mr Tainsh till you were quite certain you were to get him. It's always unlucky to count your chickens before they are hatched, but we must hope for the best."

Eila laughed merrily, and said, "We are all at cross purposes, mamma; how very, very droll! Mr Tainsh is a worthy man, but he entirely forgot his place when he proposed to me; and really I'm afraid I can't give him another chance, for I'm engaged to Mr Bertrand Cameron, mamma."

Such a possibility had, of course, been from time to time before Mrs M'Killop's mind, but it had not materially entered into her calculations; and now the full light of the actual fact suddenly bursting upon her had a bewildering effect, and she plumped down upon the sofa, only able to ejaculate "Mr Cameron!"

Her brain was not very quick, so the advantages and disadvantages of the affair were not at once clearly before her; but in her present frame of mind anything that was pleasant to Eila was painful to her, and therefore the intelligence was decidedly disagreeable on a first hearing. Nor did it improve on consideration; for then she remembered that Bertrand had been, in a sort of secondary way, designed for Morna; and, now that he might have been utilised, here was this eternal marplot pouncing upon him.

"Of course! as a matter of course!" she said to herself, bitterly.

Then, as she sat silent, and Eila ran on with her story of how Bertrand had spoken to papa, and how pleased papa had been, and what "handsome, noble promises" papa had made, it dawned upon her that the financial aspect of the affair was far from satisfactory. "Hampering our income," she said to herself, "with a large allowance just now, and a third of his fortune to go to the minx after his death! I should like to know what he means to do for me. I'm to be put off with a trumpery jointure, I suppose; no ready money, no capital—nothing to leave to my family."

Such was the current of her thoughts, the only offset against the disadvantages of Eila's engagement—that Eila would no longer be an inmate of the house—seeming, for the moment, not at all adequate. It was not to be expected, therefore, that her congratulations should be very cordial.

"It is my duty to wish you well in your new life, Eila," she said, "but I cannot say you deserve well. Anything worse than your conduct to Mr Tainsh I do not remember. If *I* was your own mother, I would let you know my mind freely, I can tell you."

"And as you are not, dear mamma, suppose we say no more about it?"

"I would let you know how I despise double games, and false encouragements, and idle heartless flirtings; and that I think eyes that roll always for admiration, are not the eyes" (rather losing herself in her metaphor) "to be helpmeets to husbands, or take up and bear a share of life's trials, and so forth. As to Mr Cameron, I have nothing to say against him; but he is young, he is very young, he is far too young. Men are all fickle, especially very young men. Probably he will repent; if he jilts you, you will regret Mr Tainsh. People will tell him it is a bad match—plebeian (you know, Eila, your origin is not like Morna's and mine)—and that will set his pride up, or his uncle's pride—they are a proud race—and then where will you be? Take friendly advice, and don't be sanguine; say nothing to any one about it at present, and then the fall won't be so deep."

"Now, mamma, what more could you have said if I *had* been your own child? Your kindness is really more than I had any right to expect."

"Act on my advice, Eila, and you will always find me glad to advise you."

"I know I shall—I know I shall!" cried Eila, leaving the room; adding, outside the room, " and I shall always be happy to receive it when it is as spiteful, for that tells me how bitterly you feel my happiness."

CHAPTER XIX.

As yesterday had been a day of proposals, so to-day had been one of interviews; and there was that sort of mystery and hush in the establishment which seems perceptible and communicable even to outsiders during a domestic crisis, when the servants lower their voices and move stealthily about the house, when the closing of a door is fraught with mystery, and the jangling of a bell suggests a *dénouement*. It had been a day of interviews, and the list of them was brought to a close when Mrs M'Killop had "interviewed" her lord and master. That he was her lord and master in any other than a poetical and honorary sense of the term, Mrs M'Killop did not believe, and would have denied with indignation, convinced as she was that all things in the family commonwealth were regulated according to her ordinances. Her husband's quietness and self-absorption fostered this delusion, as did his avoidance of dispute with regard to unimportant matters. And, after all, a fussy, violent disposition *is* very apt to carry its point in non-essentials. Common-sense weighs the value of time and tissue, in combating for it, against the worth of a trifling victory. In ninety-nine cases out of a hundred, such victories are not worth the trouble of achieving them; and as the fussy and violent temperament, which is fussy and violent upon every subject, loses all sense of proportion, and values the fact of conquest far more than the point gained, the one-per-cent of defeat, when common-sense does show fight on an important point, seems no more than the exception proving the rule. Hence Mrs M'Killop considered her sway absolute, and flattered herself that if she determined to make her husband withdraw his consent to his daughter's marriage, there would be no difficulty in carrying her point. She had thought the matter well over, however, and had eventually decided that it would be rather like cutting off her nose to spite her face, if she ran through the arrangement. "I will allow it to go on, but I will frighten him in the first place," was the decision which she carried to her husband's business-room.

The expression of majestic gloom with which, in fulfilment of this programme, she confronted Mr M'Killop, seemed, however, to be strangely lost upon him. He met it, to her astonishment, with a look of tranquil, cheerful brightness, perfectly unusual to him; and at once, with an equally unusual volubility, proceeded to unfold to her what he called "the good news." To this expression his wife took immediate exception; considered the news very bad—even deplorable; and indicated that she had by no means decided upon giving *her* sanction to the match. And here she found, like many other sovereigns, that there is some point where the will of the subject cannot be overridden. In the quietest way possible, her husband pointed out that it was no affair of hers, and that his decision was perfectly independent and final.

"I am sorry," he added, "that you don't see the matter as I do, but that is my only regret in the matter. If you only knew what a happiness it is to me—what a burden it lifts off my mind—what a burden of——," here he checked himself for a moment, and went on : " you would be glad, I think, to further it."

No argument could have been less telling upon Mrs M'Killop; with any little advantage as to comfort which it might bring to her personally, the marriage brought her a world of immediate chagrin and vexation, not to speak of possible disadvantages in the future; and to be told that it made her husband happier than he had been for years, was not, under the circumstances, a feature in the project likely to move such a nature to zealous co-operation, altogether apart from the unseemly and unwonted refusal to recognise her sovereign rights which had gone before. She was, moreover, not at all certain that M'Killop had any right to independent sources of happiness; and as to lifting a burden from his mind—what burden was it? and what business had he to have a burden without her sanction? Altogether, she was exasperated, and set herself to undermine, by every unpleasant suggestion, the rebellious satisfaction in which her husband was indulging. In this way she dwelt upon the youth of the suitor; the short acquaintance between him and his betrothed; the fickleness of unripe manhood; the folly of rash engagements; the almost certain misery of marriages entered into before the contracting parties "knew their own minds;" the extreme improbability of its ever coming to anything; the probable opposition of his family, and their reasonable suspicion that Bertrand had been entrapped for the sake of his prospects.

M'Killop was not to be moved by all these stock considerations, and parried the last by remarking that, when the fortune he designed for Eila was considered, mercenary motives could hardly be attributed to him; and on Mrs M'Killop disinterestedly remarking that she thought the destined provision excessive and unfair to—to others—she meant his son, of course — he cried out, with inexplicable energy, that he would double it rather than see the marriage fall through.

The tormentor was nonplussed; and setting this flight down to the rampagiousness of obstinacy glorying in a first success, she resolved that her husband should find, by a hundred petty discomfitures, that a second would be dearly bought. She had all but emptied her quiver of annoyances, and shot the last shaft without expecting it to tell. It did so, however, and, to her surprise, with marvellous effect; and was delivered on this wise :—

"All I can say is, that Eila's conduct has been most improper throughout; I don't know what the neighbourhood will say."

"I can't say I have noticed the impropriety; and I don't think the neighbours are likely to interest themselves in the matter, one way or other, considering we know no one in the neighbourhood."

"I alluded to this sad business with Mr Tainsh."

"Mr Tainsh! what sad business?"

"Oh! you may pretend not to know, but it won't do; and Mr Tainsh is not the man to conceal his wrongs—his cruel injuries; Eila's name will be blasted—*blasted.*"

"Good gracious! Mrs M'Killop," cried her husband, starting up in visible agitation; "what do you mean? No more riddles, if you please."

"No riddles, M'Killop; plain, sad truth,

seen by all the world. Do you mean to tell me you didn't see that Mr Tainsh was in love with Eila?"

"I did not; he never told me; I never noticed it."

"He told *me*, however, M'Killop."

"Well?"

"'Well?' you take it coolly, upon my word! Yes, M'Killop, he was in love with her; she did all in her power, used every device and art, to make him love her, under my eyes, and I saw it; under your nose, and it seems you didn't even suspect it!"

"Well?"

"'Well' again! Is that conduct worthy of a Christian female, M'Killop?"

"She couldn't propose to him, you know, Elisabeth."

"Oh! I wouldn't be too sure of that, if it had suited her; but it didn't suit her, and it wasn't necessary, for she made him propose to her."

"No!"

"Yes, indeed; just to have the pleasure of refusing him, insulting him, telling him that he was too low for her notice; ridiculing his honest love, M'Killop, as an offering only fit for a dairymaid, and an outrage to her. Her father's friend had a right to expect different treatment. When we came upon the scene of the refusal, it was plain to me that she was *violently* insulting Mr Tainsh."

"Good heavens! I had no idea of all this; it is very bad—very painful. I would give anything that it had not happened."

"No man can forgive such an insult," continued Mrs M'Killop, in solemn didactic tones; "and no man can forget the shocking way she threw herself at young Cameron. Mr Tainsh will have his revenge. He has gone away in wrath—in fury—in madness," she continued, her imagination warming to the work, "and he is now telling all the world how things are carried on here—how sensible men are insulted and befooled, and young fools entrapped by designing minxes. A nice character we shall have! and my poor dear Morna will suffer. There, M'Killop, you needn't be so very triumphant about your fine marriage. It won't sound so well, reported by that injured man."

"Good God!" repeated M'Killop, pacing the room in great agitation, "I wouldn't for the world Tainsh was offended or hurt in any way. There's no saying——he might——I like Tainsh——I owe him kindnesses, you see. I wouldn't have Tainsh made unfriendly—that is, I would not be unfriendly to Tainsh for any consideration. Are you sure he is feeling it in this way?"

"Certain; he is simply maddened."

"Then we must make it up to him. I must write—you must write—Eila shall write—we'll all write, and apologise; or I'll go and see him this very day. I'll follow him, and tell him it was beyond my control—that I knew nothing of it. *You* know that; you can tell him that. I can swear it with a safe conscience. Tainsh has reason—Tainsh has common-sense. He can't resent it on me. No, no; but something must be done at once."

All the brightness had faded from M'Killop's face, and a look of anxiety and distress had replaced it, as he moved about the room in short, quick, uncertain strides, betraying extreme nervous agitation in every gesture. His wife looked at him in astonishment; the symptoms he betrayed appeared to her to be out of all proportion to their cause, especially in so phlegmatic a man. She felt that she had overdone her part. Having merely meant to vex and irritate him, she found that she had roused him into a kind of frenzy—a frenzy perfectly unaccountable to her, but there it was; and it was now necessary for her, having roused it, to undo the work she had done, and to prevent action being taken, which, as she knew, would only place them all in a ridiculous and humiliating light before Mr Tainsh.

To soothe her lord she found no easy task, even with the half-admission that her feelings had carried her away into exaggeration; and all the success she achieved before leaving was the extortion of a promise to suspend action for the moment—and with this she was fain to be content. Her interview had been altogether a failure — it had left her entirely baffled; and there was a mystery about her husband's whole conduct in the matter from first to last, which piqued her with the idea of a secret motive—secret from her. If she had had any doubt on the subject, it was set at rest, a few minutes after the close of their conversation, when, going quietly into his room to look for something which she had left behind, she found him standing with his back to the door, still in the same attitude, and heard him mutter to himself—

"Good God! have I found the chance, after all these years? Have I found the means—simple and harmless—of setting all to rights—and only to lose it?"

"What chance? setting what to rights, M'Killop?" cried his wife, unable to restrain herself.

Her husband turned fiercely upon her, with a look she had never seen in his face before, and, quivering with rage, ordered her from his sight, with a torrent of imprecations that came with startling effect from so unlikely a source, and revealed to her, for the first time, that, under that quiet and almost sanctimonious exterior, there lay, unknown and unguessed by her, a second life, from which these utterances came. She fled from the room in real terror —and from that date her theory of government was revolutionised. If yesterday—the feast of proposals—had terminated in general discomfiture and gloom, so to-day the resulting interviews had, after all, left matters in no more satisfactory condition. As there had been only two in the *dramatis personæ* of yesterday for whom the action of the piece went smoothly, so to-day there were still only two. Tainsh and Duncanson, indeed, had withdrawn their contributions to the dismal department, but their places had been supplied by Mr and Mrs M'Killop, who were now looking their parts to a marvel. Such were Pigott's sentiments, as he surveyed the party at dinner, not without disapprobation.

"As for these two idiots," he said to himself, alluding to Eila and Bertrand, "of course they are too ineffably happy not to be silent; and although the consciousness that there *are* two people ineffably happy in a room has a depressing effect, still it needn't be so bad as this. One would have thought the parent-birds would have liked it, but it doesn't seem so. What's the matter with old M'Killop? he's piano enough in general, but to-day he looks as if he was going to be knouted. And the other old miscreant—even her voice would be a relief. How red her face is! perhaps she's been drinking, and daren't trust herself to speak. And Morna too—looking as if she was at a funeral. Upon my life, it *is* rather too hard upon me : conversation is not my line, but one has a right to expect it from others."

It certainly was not a convivial occasion. Eila and Bertrand found it satisfactory enough, but it did strike even their preoccupation that M'Killop was not quite the ideal of the delighted parent he had represented himself in the morning to be. Bertrand had feared that there might be some demonstrative congratulations when the party met at dinner—slynesses and vulgar rallyings on the part of Mrs M'Killop — a speech, perhaps, from M'Killop (in the morning he had appeared capable of anything), and, at all events, a pretty exuberant marking of the auspicious occasion. But there was not an allusion made to the subject which must have been uppermost in the mind of every one ; and, as Pigott noted with intense disapprobation, " the old curmudgeon didn't even pull out his champagne." As the dinner passed, so passed the rest of the evening. Morna was in her own room, making preparations for her journey of the morrow, and did not appear in the drawing-room till the party were about to break up for the night. M'Killop sat silent, staring at the newspaper, and

Pigott found Mrs M'Killop so wild in her play at their habitual *ecarté*, that he pocketed his winnings with a recurrence of the suspicion which had crossed his mind at dinner. As for the lovers—Bertrand had left the dining-room immediately after the ladies, and very soon he and Eila were out across the terrace and away among the woods, where time, place, and circumstance were all forgotten, and whence they did not return till the darkness had long fallen, when they crept guiltily back, anticipating a domestic storm. The storm-fiend was contemptuously quiescent, however, merely remarking, " Since you *have* returned," as if the contingency was but remotely probable, " and as Morna makes a very early start to-morrow, perhaps we had better go to bed."

" An early start, Miss Grant !" cried Bertrand ; " are you going away ? Where to ? not for long, I hope ?"

" Three questions !" said Morna. " Yes, Mr Cameron, I *am* going away to-morrow morning. I am going to join my aunts at Glenfail ; how long I shall be away I don't quite know, but I don't think it is at all likely that I shall be back before you leave ; so it is good-night and good-bye ;" and she held out her hand.

"I am very sorry," said Bertrand, warmly—"very sorry indeed ; but perhaps we shall meet in England ; in any case——"

He wished to make some allusion to their future connection, but paused, and she finished his sentence for him :—

"In any case we shall perhaps meet some time or other. Good-bye."

"Good-bye," said Bertrand, feeling some disappointment that one whom he regarded with such friendly feelings should have made no allusion to present circumstances ; but so it was, and so the party broke up. That night Bertrand indited the momentous letter to his uncle, asking that potentate to sanction his happiness—a mere formal compliment, he felt it to be, for the veriest simpleton, he assured himself, would at once recognise the advantages of such an alliance ; and his uncle was no simpleton — far from it. So the letter was written, and Bertrand sat down with his friend to be jolly, feeling that all he had now to do was to exercise a little patience for the consummation of his happiness. His friend was not in the best of tempers, and, indeed, much the reverse of sympathetic, entirely declining to believe in the rapture with which Sir Roland was expected to receive the intelligence.

"Nobody in his senses," he said, "could think it anything but foolish. The young lady of course is—don't look so fierce, Bertrand—an angel; but the parents—well, it is as well that Sir Roland is not to have a photograph of them and their manners when he sits in judgment on the case. I always told you you would make a fool of yourself."

"You forget yourself, Pigott."

"No disparagement to the *beaux yeux*, my dear fellow—quite the reverse; and, after all, if you like to put your neck in a halter at twenty-two—*ce n'est pas mon affaire*. But I'll tell you what *is* my affair; and that is, that this is all deuced slow for me. If I had only foreseen what was to turn up, you wouldn't have caught me going partners with you, I can tell you."

"I think it's as jolly as possible."

"Of course you do, you imbecile; but do you think it's jolly for me—all this mystery, and love-making, and glum looks?—hang me!

if one mightn't as well be at Colney Hatch, in the melancholy department. It's simply infernal—that's what it is—and I think you've used me abominably ill."

Bertrand laughed good-humouredly at his friend's vigorous sally, and answered, " But even to look at the matter from your own prosaic, practical point of view, Eila is to have fifty thousand pounds."

" There you go—self, self, self. Fifty thousand pounds! fifty thousand angels of darkness, or of light. That doesn't make *my* billet here the pleasanter; that doesn't give *me* a sane companion to speak to and shoot with; it doesn't make Mrs M'Killop's vulgarity less offensive to *me;* and she's almost my only resource left now, now Morna is going away, who was by far the best of the whole party."

" With an exception," interpolated Bertrand.

" Oh, hang it! I have no patience with you or anybody or anything," vociferated Pigott. " I've lost an autumn; the same money would have paid for a share in the yacht, and the Norway fishing with Ridley; and here I am, shut up in a confounded prison, surrounded with moping lunatics and detestable old harridans; and the grub isn't so good as it was; and I am sometimes thirsty at dinner for ten minutes—(perhaps, now you're in the firm, you'll speak about *that*)—and because old Blowhard happens to be in the blues, that's no reason why he shouldn't pass the wine. And just look at that wood — green and smoky! By George! I'll be off, and claim half the money back!"

"I never saw you in such a vile temper, Pigott. I'm sorry you're annoyed. I daresay it *is* slow for you, but I'll try to be more amusing. As for the other grievance, I think that is only the suggestion of an evil temper. It *is* a bore, Morna's going away; she would have kept you alive."

"She was getting as bad as the rest; and no wonder, in such a hole as this."

"By the by, I *did* notice that she wasn't so cheery latterly."

"Oh! you noticed *that*, did you?"

"Yes—she was almost cross sometimes, I thought; and she didn't even congratulate me —odd, wasn't it?"

"Perhaps."

"What do you mean?"

" Perhaps she had her reasons."

" You're very mysterious."

" Am I ?"

" To change the subject, Tainsh apologised."

" Without a thrashing ?"

" Yes."

" And Duncanson?"

" I had no quarrel with him."

" He had with you, though."

" I can't make out why."

" No ?"

" Can you ?"

" Ha! ha!"

" As you can't take the trouble to speak like a reasonable being, I'll go to bed. Good-night, and a better temper to you."

" Whispers of angels make music in your dreams, oh unconscionable dolt!"

CHAPTER XX.

Morna's room adjoined the business-room of Mr M'Killop, and when the party broke up this evening, she was surprised to hear that, contrary to his wont, he came thither instead of going straight up to bed. Her attention was specially drawn to this by the fact that, apparently, he had come neither to read nor to write, but to occupy himself—singularly enough at that hour of the night—in walking up and down the apartment. The house was badly deafened, so that sounds from the next room came to Morna's very distinctly, and in this way she was able to remark that M'Killop was walking up and down, in the manner of a man who debates some subject with himself, with a good deal of agitation and hesitancy, his steps being now quick, short, and undecided, now long, slow, and steady.

This was continued so long that Morna's attention was withdrawn from it, until the footsteps ceased to sound, and she heard the doors of a large cabinet unlocked, and the hinges creak as they were opened. The rustling of papers was then audible, and even some muttered ejaculations of her step-father's—the sense of which, however, she did not, as she did not wish to, catch. At last he spoke out —quite loud—louder than in ordinary conversation, so that to overhear him became unavoidable.

"No, no : it cannot be wrong. Where *is* the harm? Simply to postpone—that is not to defeat justice. Not at all. It will be all for the best. I will keep the paper *in case;* while it exists, no eventual harm can be done. The letter may be destroyed, though—and here it is——"

Morna heard the sound of a paper being torn up, and almost at the same instant there was a sort of choking cry and the noise of a heavy fall; and, running in, she found Mr M'Killop lying insensible on the floor. She obtained assistance without alarming her mother, and in a few minutes he sufficiently regained consciousness to enable him to forbid a doctor, or even his wife, being sent for. When he was so far recovered, and had been removed to his own dressing-room, which was at hand, Morna left him; and noticing, as she passed the business-room, that the doors of the cabinet stood open, she went in, locked them, took the key, and was about to extinguish the light when her eye fell on a letter torn in half, lying near the spot where Mr M'Killop had fallen.

"This," she thought to herself, "must be what I heard him tear; and it certainly was some agitation connected with this letter that brought on his illness. Perhaps he didn't know what he was doing when he tore it up; he was seized at the very moment; in any case, it can do no harm if I take it, and send it back to him with his keys." She took it accordingly, and went to her room, resolving, since she was to start early, to enclose it to him with a note explaining under what circumstances she had found it. In the process of folding the torn letter, however, her eye was involuntarily attracted, as eyes — even the honestest—may be, by an expression in it; an expression of such interest, that under the influence, as it were, of an irresistible fascination, she read on, and before reflection on the impropriety of what she was doing came back to her, she shared with Mr M'Killop a secret which it deeply distressed her to possess, and which it would no doubt still more shock him to find her in possession of.

"What am I to do?" she exclaimed, in desperation; but she was spared the trouble of further reflection, for at this moment a message came from Mr M'Killop requesting her to come to him at once.

She found him lying on his bed: he had quite recovered consciousness, but was looking prostrate, and spoke in a feeble voice. "I am very sorry, Morna," he said, "to trouble you at this late hour, but I understand you were the first to come to me when I was taken ill?"

"Yes, I was."

"Did you notice if the doors of my cabinet were open?"

"Yes, they were."

"I am still too giddy to move without danger of bringing on another attack, and I don't like to trust a servant; will you kindly go and lock it, and bring me the keys?"

"I have locked it already; and I have the keys: here they are."

"Many thanks to you, Morna; this is most prudent, and like yourself. I rather fancy I was destroying a paper at the time I was taken ill; whether I had quite destroyed it or not, I don't know: did you happen to see anything of the sort lying about the floor?"

"Yes, Mr M'Killop, I did."

"Perhaps you would take the trouble to pick up the fragments and bring them to me? It is an important letter, and should be thoroughly destroyed."

"I have the letter all here, Mr M'Killop."

"You really are the most sensible girl in the world."

"Stay a moment before you compliment me; I have read it."

"Read it!" cried M'Killop, in a voice of horror and amazement; "do you call that honour?"

After this no word of anger or reproach escaped him; he lay still, pale, with a look of collapse; and it was with difficulty that his trembling lips faltered the few words he wished to say.

"No," replied Morna, "I do not; and even now I cannot understand how I came to read it. Some words which caught my eye at the commencement of the letter so startled me, that I began involuntarily; and what I read so absorbed me, that I went on to the end—almost, I may say, unconsciously."

"You are conscious of the secret it contains, however?"

"I am; and however I may regret the means by which I obtained possession of it, I cannot regret that I am; because it would seem that you were abandoning an act of justice you had once intended to perform."

"No, no; you must not go by appearances in this case; and surely you would not make use of information so obtained?"

"Why not?"

"It would be dishonourable."

"Is it honourable to screen dishonour? My morals may be all wrong; but I can't bring myself to see that."

"Morna, I have been kind to you; I have wished always to be very kind to you."

"Yes, Mr M'Killop, you have—and I am grateful; but that cannot affect this matter. In a question of right or wrong I cannot let my judgment be influenced by considerations of feeling merely; and as to the means by which I have become possessed of your secret, —if I heard—overheard—one man confiding to another the scheme of some terrible wickedness he meant to commit—a murder, for instance—would it be dishonourable in me to make use of the intelligence I had obtained by involuntary eavesdropping to save a man's life?"

"This has nothing to do with a murder."

"No, but the same principle applies to it. I am a thousand times sorry, as I have said, for the way I got the information, but, having got it, I will use it, unless you act yourself; I could not do otherwise."

"Listen, Morna; it is a very intricate story; I promise you I will put all to rights; I swear to you that it is my most anxious wish to do so; but unreasonable haste may ruin all—*all;* involve innocent people in the consequences of guilt, and even compromise my character. You would be both rash and unfair in acting without me; and though you might fancy that you were doing an act of justice, you would in reality be doing injustice ten times greater. You cannot doubt, under the circumstances in which I am placed, that it is my interest as well as my duty to see justice done."

"I certainly cannot see that your interest and your duty are opposed to each other; but what interest you can have had all along——"

"That is nothing to the purpose. Leave it to me; it will take a little time, but right *shall* be done, you may depend upon it. One thing—it must not transpire before Eila's marriage with Mr Cameron; that is indispensable. Allow me" (as she was going to interrupt him) "to be the best judge of my own plans and ideas, and to add that I see no reason why you should threaten an honest man with pressure to be honest."

"Pardon me, Mr M'Killop—I only see a wrong existing; and if you tell me that a little delay is necessary that full justice should be done, I am satisfied."

"Till after the marriage, Morna."

"Very well; but if—supposing—that is—

well, I *must* say it—supposing you should die in the mean time?"

"In that case you are at liberty to disclose what you have discovered, and you will find full proof of what that letter stated, in the top drawer, on the right-hand side of the cabinet; there it shall remain in the mean time."

"I shall never be easy till it is off my mind."

"Nevertheless, having possessed yourself of my secret—only to a certain extent—you are bound not to use it so as to hurt me, while others' interests are on the way to be established."

"I will not; but I hope there will not be much delay. Good-bye."

"Good-bye. Do not think ill of me; believe that any bad impression of me which this affair may produce, will be absolutely removed when the truth is fully made known. Ah, Morna! you don't know how much I am to be pitied."

"Any one with such a secret is to be pitied." And then she added, touched by the forlorn aspect of the man — "I *am* very sorry for you, Mr M'Killop. I cannot believe that you would do anything wrong or unjust, voluntarily and wittingly. Good-bye. I hope you will take care of yourself. It is the agitation of this miserable affair that has made you ill." And so they separated.

"She will require management," muttered M'Killop, when he was again alone.

"Surely I *must* be right in believing that he is honest," thought Morna.

Thus ended the last of all the day's interviews—a pretty mysterious one too ; and perhaps after this some of us would be inclined in meeting M'Killop to button our pockets in case—only in case—of accidents.

CHAPTER XXI.

We shall not dwell any longer in detail upon the remainder of Bertrand's and Pigott's stay at Cairnarvoch.

For the former, the time passed all too quickly, every day unfolding new charms in the object of his love, every hour increasing his enchantment, till even the ideal of his early worship looked, in the cold distance of the past, but a dim, imperfect shadow, compared with the bright reality now flooding his life with sunshine. As for the others, Pigott's temper, which, as a rule, was eminently equable, soon regained its tone; the weather was glorious, the sport good—for him two grand consolations; so that he even recovered some of his original semi-enthusiasm for the place and its amusements.

The cloud soon passed from Mr M'Killop's

brow. Tainsh had shown no malice; so far from carrying the fiery cross of denunciation and slander about the country, as predicted by Mrs M'Killop, he had written a cordial note of congratulation on the news "conveyed to him by Mr Cameron," and M'Killop beamed upon the young couple, and seemed to await as impatiently as they the arrival of Sir Roland's *fiat*. Mrs M'Killop could not, from her very nature, remain long in cold abstraction, and ere long her noisy tongue clattered with all its wonted energy: her secret sorrows and disappointments were, no doubt, assuaged by the prospect of excitement in store—a *trousseau* to superintend—the *éclat* of a marriage, and all the bustle, movement, noise, and display therewith connected: altogether, the latter weeks of the Cairnarvoch campaign passed blessedly for some, tranquilly for others, and tolerably at least for all. But the most liberal "leave" must have an end, and with the second week of October that of Bertrand and Pigott came to a close; and the lover had to turn his back upon his love, and return to his duty; and never was the old antagonism between love and duty more keenly appreciated than now by him, as he mooned through his daily occupations in a somnambulistic way, wondering to find everything so changed—the joys of the barracks so flat, the duties so stale, the companionship so wearily vapid and unprofitable.

Sir Roland's answer was not expected for three months, and in the event of its being favourable it was decided that the marriage should take place immediately after its arrival. The delay and the separation would probably have been irksome and trying to most men; but to Bertrand, who thought and felt and acted, all, so to speak, in the superlative degree, the weariness of this interval appeared to be something without a parallel. What had formerly constituted his social pleasures now offered no distraction, and occupations that had once been full of interest afforded him no relief. Garrison convivialities were coarse orgies; garrison duty a solemn farce; the funniest man in the regiment was a dreary buffoon, and the smartest officer a peddling prig. Looking thus on his surroundings with a jaundiced eye, his surroundings soon began to return the compliment; for where there is a large circle of cheery companionship to choose from, it is not to be expected that men whose object it is to live merrily all the days of their lives, should trouble themselves to coax a moody man into good-fellowship. So Bertrand dropped into a state of isolation strangely in contrast with his former position in the regiment, and had a weary, fretful time of it, his mind inverted and staring at its own discontent, morn, noon, and night. In all the twenty-four hours there was but one gleam of sunshine for him, and that was when the post came in and brought Eila's daily epistle—for a daily epistle was of course necessary to keep the lovers properly posted up in the thermometric readings of each other's hearts——; and charming letters Eila wrote, full of life and sparkle, freely interspersed with the essential element, and, one-half at least, devoted to the discussion of Bertrand's merits, moral, intellectual, and physical. They were most satisfactory, and they did satisfy their recipient for about an hour, after which he began to look forward to the next, with a full recurrence of the restless cravings and longings of the lovesick.

Pigott was his only resource in the way of

society. He had always, as we know, been Bertrand's very special friend; and now the merit of knowing *her* procured for him a monopoly of the lover's company—a distinction which poor Pigott sometimes found to be rather oppressive.

"A little of that kind of thing goes a long way with most men," he complained pathetically to the Mess one day; "and every one knows it is not in my line. I would do a deal for Bertrand, but he *does* become maddening at times—simply maddening. His conversation has become a sort of—what do you call it? what they sing at the end of the Psalms? yes—a doxology; and he won't let me off a single 'Amen.' If the marriage doesn't come off soon, I'll do something desperate. I believe my reason is beginning to totter; as for my digestive organs, they are simply nowhere. I dream at nights. I dreamt last night that the marriage was coming off. I was the groomsman, and my duty was to carry a haggis to church under each arm, and to see that the bride and bridegroom each disposed of one before the ring was put on. That shows what a state I must be in."

Notwithstanding all this, however, Pigott was, on the whole, very patient with his friend, and only showed himself otherwise now and then; on which occasions he would viciously point out the absurdity of expecting Sir Roland to give his consent to the marriage, or dilate with a great deal of powerful word-painting on the idiosyncrasies of Mr and Mrs M'Killop.

Then Bertrand would flare up, and there would be a row—such rows as always happen between men who are too much shut up together—and then a reconciliation, and so forth.

The time went past, however, somehow, and the winter crept on. The M'Killops went down to Edinburgh, partly from stress of weather, and partly because they wished to lose not a moment in commencing arrangements for the wedding, when the "mere matter of form" arrived from the antipodes. It was Bertrand's earnest prayer in all his letters, that these arrangements might be proceeded with in anticipation—the *trousseau* procured, the day named, even the guests bidden—and nothing left to be done but start for church, and live happy ever after, as soon as Sir Roland dropped the flag. It was his pet grievance, for ever dinned into his friend's tingling ears, that this prayer was not complied with; to which Pigott, when out of temper, would reply, that " old M'Killop was not half such a fool as he looked, and knew perfectly well that a second-hand *trousseau* and a stale wedding-cake were about the most unsaleable forms which portable property could assume."

At last the period of suspense came to a close; the eventful day arrived; the colonial mail came in, and Bertrand found on his table the unmistakable despatch, directed in his uncle's handwriting—the order of release from purgatory—the "Open Sesame" before which the gates of Hymen were to expand.

Quivering with excitement, he seized the fateful missive, tore it open, and read as follows :—

"*1st December* 18—.

" DEAR BERTRAND,—I duly received your letter of the 12th September, but as the same mail brought me a communication from an individual who professes an interest in your welfare (though he desires to remain incognito), containing statements bearing upon the matter of your letter, I have delayed my reply to you till I could verify these statements, which I have been enabled to do by communicating with correspondents in a neighbouring colony. Looking only to your own letter, requesting my consent to your marriage with a Miss M'Killop,—the daughter of a person with whom, as far as I can make out, you have been boarding in Scotland during the autumn,—I should have been inclined to say, first, that your application to me ought properly to have preceded your addresses to the lady in question, your own means not enabling you, without my assistance, to carry out any engagement of the sort. Knowing, however, that your disposition is eminently rash and impulsive, I might have been inclined to look upon this error with some leniency, had the step you propose to take not been open to the gravest objection in every particular. That at your age, in your profession, and with your *vague* prospects, you should dream of matrimony at all, argues a tolerably advanced stage of folly; but that you should gravely propose to ally yourself with a nameless nobody, and thereby sacrifice any advantage of connection which you now have, or might possibly acquire, really appears to be insanity pure and simple. With nothing, then, to go upon but your own letter, I should have unhesitatingly withheld my consent, and warned you to look for no countenance or assistance from me in the event of your declining to abandon the engagement. But if these were my views merely on your own statement of the case, you may imagine what they became, when I learned from your friend the fact—the *horrible* fact—that the person, whose daughter you propose to make your wife, has actually been a convicted felon, and has undergone, in a colony adjacent to this, a term of penal servitude. There is no possible doubt as to the identity of the man. Dismiss any such idea which your own wishes might suggest. I have ascertained the facts of the case. I neither speak nor act upon some light, hearsay evidence, and what I assert, you may thoroughly depend upon. Under these circumstances, it is idle for me to discuss the matter. I can only hope—and indeed I can scarcely doubt—that you will assure me, by the return mail, that you were ignorant of the stigma attaching to the family you propose to ally yourself with, that you recoil with horror from an engagement contracted in ignorance of it, and could not for an instant look upon such an obstacle as otherwise than insurmountable. I can scarcely doubt, I say, that you will write to me at once in this sense.

"But there must be no sort of misconception on your part, as to how I shall act, if unfortunately I should be wrong, and if, in one of those flights of wrong-headed romance in which you seem occasionally to indulge, you should still venture to think of such a disgraceful connection—led away, perhaps, by specious protestations of injured innocence, or by the vehemence of your misplaced attachment: therefore I tell you plainly, that unless you furnish me with a prompt assurance, upon your honour, that the engagement is at an end, and that you will have no further communication with the girl, I shall cease to look upon you as a member of my family, or as interested any longer, in the remotest degree, in the destination of my property, which, under such circumstances, I have full legal power to alienate from you. I trust such stern measures will never be called for. I sincerely trust that, as a threat, they are unnecessary. I prefer to believe that the recollection of what is due to the honour of our ancient race will be alone sufficient to make you do what is right. Still it is necessary that there should be no possibility of misconception, and so I speak plainly. I look anxiously for your reply, and remain your affectionate uncle,

"ROLAND CAMERON."

Bertrand began to read this letter, standing upright at the table; as he read, his colour changed, his eyes became dilated, and his lips were tightly compressed; but when he came to the passage "has actually been a convicted felon," he paused, stared wildly about him, and sank down upon a chair, with such a cry of anguish as can only come from a heart stricken with some sudden, excruciating pain. Still he read on—almost mechanically—to the end, and then the paper fell from his hand, as though he had been paralysed.

A numb stupor came over his mind; his consciousness seemed to be pent in by walls of thick, impenetrable cloud; and the pressure of a darkness that could be felt, weighed upon him with an indefinite sense of overwhelming misery. He was stunned; he was conscious only of utter pain and misery; everything else was confused and indefinite; and it was only after a long interval, and slowly, that from this chaos, the actual calamity which had befallen him shaped itself out in clear, inexorable reality.

Every graceful attribute, every charm of mind or of person, which Eila possessed, had been so wrought up by Bertrand's love and poetic fancy, that she had become to him a being inhabiting the earth, indeed—mysteriously inhabiting the earth—yet not of it; a being too ethereal and pure to be affected by the sordid details of everyday existence, a unique creation, "a floweret of Eden," upon which the serpent's trail could never pass. All associations of common life that accidentally obtruded themselves, from time to time, in any sort of juxtaposition with the thought of her, jarred upon him painfully, as if the flow of a harmony had been suddenly interrupted by some intolerable discord. Not the least of these had been, at first, the circumstance that she possessed a father to whose earthly characteristics it was impossible to be blind; but, after all, he was an unobtrusive person; and, what with habit and daily contemplation, what with some instinctive sympathy with a natural affection which he felt that Eila must entertain towards this detrimental parent, he had got to look upon him as rather negatively an evil, than a positive profanation of the object of his worship. Thus the fact of her paternity had hung, like a cloud indeed, but remotely, on the far-away horizon of his otherwise sunbright heaven. But now came this disillusionising fact, breaking, as by a counter-spell, the magic circle with which his imagination had hedged her in; and there was she, whom in his fastidious devotion he would have guarded from contact with aught that was prosaic, were it never so innocent—there was she, the prismatic nimbus that enveloped her, reft and dissipated, standing revealed in indissoluble association with all that was vilest and most degrading. Bertrand contemplated this, and was torn with the agony of a struggle between the different elements which go to make up what the world calls "Love." We all know how little there often is of the pure essence in that mysterious compound; how Vanity, Egotism, Self-love, and Self-interest, calling Fancy to their aid, can put on the graceful semblance of the passion, and pass, even self-deceiving, for its reality; and how often the strongest analytic test can scarcely disintegrate the counterfeit. To such a test was Bertrand's love now exposed. Richly overlaid, and glittering with beautiful illusions, it was cast into the alembic: stern was the ordeal, and mortal the pain, as the fire burned, and, one by one, each baser ingredient turned into refuse. Mortal, indeed, was the pain; but Bertrand's love was pure and tender and true, and, if it came forth stripped of many a grace and charm, it was still intact in its strong truth and tenderness. Pride, indeed, spoke out to him of contaminated blood, and chivalrous traditions cancelled by alliance with disgrace. Duty and Prudence counselled obedience to his uncle's wishes, and whispered of the penalties of disobedience; but all in vain.

"Did I not love her," he cried out, as if arguing the point with an antagonist—"did I not love her for her heart, for her mind, for her beauty, for her grace, for her innocence—

for all those qualities that, making up *her*, make her superior to every other woman in the world? Did I not love her, purely and disinterestedly, for herself alone? Is she altered now? The taint was on her birth when I first loved her; it made her none the less lovable when it was unsuspected; and now being known, can it alter her intrinsically? It cannot—it does not. She to whom I gave my love is still in herself the same. I loved her for herself, and nothing else. Can I abandon that love, she being unchanged? Surely never! Shall I be forsworn then to her, and to my own heart, because circumstances oppose my selfish interests to my love? Never will I be guilty of such infamy. But all the more will I take her to myself, adding tender compassion to the tender love I bear her—take her to myself, away from the contamination she is unconscious of—screen her from scorn, and show that unselfish love, when centred on an object too pure for contact with the world, can despise the world's scorn and gladly sacrifice its favours. As for my uncle, what has he been to me? What but a cold and austere monitor? Has he ever shown any feeling or affection towards me—any of the interest of a near relation—even the common interest of a mere guardian? Do I owe him a debt of gratitude for neglect and coldness? Is not this letter of his an outrage upon every sentiment of kindness and affection — the cold-blooded, hard-hearted letter of an utterly selfish man incapable of sympathy? Do I owe obedience to such a man? I owe obedience to no man in this matter, and much less to him. I own no such authority; I cast it off. I cast off every tie that is opposed to her. I sacrifice every interest that stands between her and me. I accept disinheritance. It is a small sacrifice to make for her sake. O Eila! my angel!—my own for ever!—many waters quench not love, and ours no sea of troubles shall ever overwhelm!"

And so, standing on the ruins of the temple he had reared for his divinity, he vowed that his devotion was unshaken, and that, for worse or for better, his love was hers, proof against every change and chance.

These heroic resolutions of self-abnegation, these renewed oaths of fealty to his love, did not, however, exclude a feeling that Fate had given him a bitter cup to drink; and as his mental exaltation subsided, there remained a sense of personal outrage and wrong—perfectly vague, indeed, but none the less keen on that account. It was no satisfaction to execrate his uncle—his conduct under the circumstances was perfectly inevitable; it was no more satisfactory to execrate his uncle than to heap abuse upon Fate. Eila's father, again, however execrable, was not the proximate cause of his trouble, and wrath loves to expend itself on a proximate cause, taken red-handed — in the very act. With these feelings, Bertrand set himself to read a second time his uncle's letter, and presently his eye fell upon a point that had escaped his special notice in the tumult of the first perusal. It was this :—" I received a communication from one who professes an interest in your welfare, though he desires to remain incognito."

Here was the fuel for which the fire was hungering, and fierce and sudden was the blaze of Bertrand's fury. Who was this villain—this stabber in the dark? Who was this false and forsworn friend who sought to rob him of his love? What right had he to rake up secrets that need never have come to light? to give circulation to anything that might tarnish the name of her whom he adored? True or false, it was an outrage so deep and black that blood alone could wash it out. But who was he? Who could the miscreant be?

The circle of possibilities, round which his wrath travelled like lightning, was a narrow one. Almost instantly he started up, and exclaiming, "He and no other!—it *can* be no other!" dashed wildly from the room.

CHAPTER XXII.

Captain Pigott was reposing himself in his quarters, in the interval between his return from hunting and the time to dress for mess. He was seated in the cosiest of lounging-chairs, his slippered feet resting upon a yielding footstool; and the vague half-smile upon his lips, the languid and infrequent puffs which he dealt to an expiring cigarette, the gentle drooping of his eyelids, and, now and then, a suave deflection of the head, were all symptoms that he was pleasantly coquetting with the god of slumber. Upon this tranquil scene burst Bertrand Cameron, throwing the door open with a crash that made everything in the room vibrate, and roused its occupant to wakefulness and wrath.

"Now then, Bertrand," he said, petulantly, but without looking round, as knowing that no one else could venture so to enter his sanctum, "this *is* too intolerable. I told you I was tired—I even hinted that I was bored; and I believe I was just dropping off into as nice a little doze as a man need wish for, when here you come blundering back and spoil it all. Upon my life, it's too bad! Hang it all! can't a fellow be allowed to have his quarters to himself for *one* hour?"

He spoke almost pathetically, but Bertrand answered not a word.

"Now, perhaps you'll just take yourself off again, my good fellow," continued the sybarite; "I require forty or fifty winks before mess, so you must see that you can't possibly stay here."

Still Bertrand said nothing.

Surprised at this unwonted phenomenon of silence, only broken by the deep breathing of his friend, Pigott looked round, and saw on his face an expression he had never seen there before. "Hilloa!" he cried; "why, man, what's the matter? You look as if you had seen the devil!"

Bertrand glared fiercely at him, then, holding out the fatal letter, said, in a voice broken and tremulous, " I have not seen the devil, but I have seen his handiwork, and here it is."

"Don't give it me, my dear fellow; if there is one thing I hate and detest, it is the smell of sulphur," cried Pigott, adhering to his usual system of laughing off his friend's frequent tragedies.

"Silence!" thundered Bertrand.

"Well, that's exactly what I want; so if you'll only hold your tongue, and take yourself off without further parley, we shall both be satisfied."

"Silence!" reiterated Bertrand; "this is no time for jesting."

"Quite my own sentiment; I seldom have been less inclined for anything of the sort."

"You affect to misunderstand me, but——"

"On the contrary, my dear fellow, I never yet affected to understand you at all."

"Captain Pigott, this foolery must cease; this—this letter—take it and read it; you shall—you must."

"These excitable fellows generally go mad, I believe, in the long-run; and I suppose poor Bertrand's hour has come," thought Pigott, scanning his friend's face with some anxiety, however.

Then he took the letter, deliberately unfolded and began to read it with his cold passionless air, while Bertrand traversed the room with the restless strides of some caged wild animal. A grim smile overspread the reader's features as he perused the first paragraph or two, thinking, in his cynical way, "The battered old drama of first love, of course! with all its portentous company of angels and fiends, spotless maids and sinless youths, spotted guardians and sinful parents! ha! ha! ha!" But, as he read on, his face changed, and became exceedingly grave. If this man was, as some of his brother officers alleged, selfish and cold to all the rest of the world, none of them doubted or denied that there was a warm place in his heart for Bertrand, and a regard that might even have stood the test of personal sacrifice. Feeling thus, then, for his friend—whose disposition, with all its pride, romance, and fastidiousness, he thoroughly understood—and knowing the transcendental nature of his love for Eila, he not only comprehended what a terrible blow this letter must have inflicted upon Bertrand, but felt a hearty sympathy for him. And so, when he had completed the perusal, he went up to his friend, and, laying his hand upon his shoulder, expressed what he felt sincerely, though with characteristic brevity — "I am truly sorry, my poor old fellow."

But Bertrand flung him off with indignation, crying out, "Have you no shame left? Do you dare to address me as a friend?"

"Bertrand! what are you dreaming about?" cried Pigott, in real alarm: "compose yourself; for heaven's sake, try to be calm! Things may not be so bad—it may turn out to be a calumny."

"Oh! you had not even made yourself quite certain of the truth, then, before you did me this infamous wrong?"

"Why, this is stark, staring madness! Come, come, Bertrand—be a man; come, sit down—sit down now, and try to control yourself;" and he made as if he would have taken his arm.

Bertrand started back. "Don't touch me!" he cried; "don't touch me, you vile hypocrite! you false, treacherous friend! There is no word base enough and foul enough to describe your character, and none strong enough to express my loathing for it. Madness! no, I am not mad — though, God knows, I have enough to make me so: you have done your best to madden me."

"I, Bertrand? I? How? where? when? You are dreaming—or raving. Do you know who I am?"

"Yes, I know well who and what you are. A friend, a confidant, who has betrayed both characters, and hidden himself behind an incognito to do it; the man who denounced to my uncle———"

"Stop, Cameron, stop!" cried Pigott, with a sudden change of voice and expression.

"I will *not* stop," vociferated Bertrand with great vehemence — "I will *not* stop. I say you are the man who denounced to my uncle this miserable stain upon the birth of my betrothed—wantonly, in cold blood. It was my affair; it was nothing to him. Knowing that her love was everything to me, you did it. What was the motive?—in the name of everything diabolical, what was the motive of such infernal treachery? Was it———"

"You *shall* listen to me," interrupted Pigott, "if you were twenty times a madman. I have listened to you too long; I have borne too much—a thousand times more than I could from any other man. I have borne it because I was sorry for your distress, and believed that it had bewildered your mind; but this deliberate repetition is too much. If you have your grief to nurse, I have my honour to protect. No living man shall leave such a cursed imputation upon me. It must be retracted instantly, in the first place. The wildest grief and the wildest temper are no excuse for such an outrage."

"How can I retract with the evidence of this letter before my eyes? Who else *could* it have been?"

Pigott relapsed into his passionless manner. "I see," he said, "I was wrong. I have been surprised into an informality. Pray excuse it. Of course it is not for me to argue the point, or to *prove* that your charge is false, when I have *said* that it is false. I shall leave the matter in other hands. And now let me suggest that this room is mine, and that I shall expect you to have a representative ready to meet mine with the smallest possible delay." He went to the door and opened it, but Bertrand remained motionless, staring confusedly, like a man waking from a dream. "I must beg to be left alone, Mr Cameron," said Pigott.

"Can I——" stammered Bertrand; "is it possible that—— do you positively deny that you are the man who wrote?"

"I have said all that I mean to say on the subject," said Pigott.

"Give me your honour as a gentleman."

"You forget the laws of honour and the conduct of a gentleman in asking for it: when a gentleman denies a thing, he does not stoop to any more binding form."

"O Pigott!" burst out Bertrand, "I have been under a delusion—I see it now—I have wronged you. It is I that have violated friendship. Forgive me; I see it now. This horrible grief has confused all my thoughts. It is more than I can bear. Forgive me."

Pigott bore no malice, but he was ashamed of having been surprised into a display of violent emotion—almost into what he called "a fit of Bertrand's theatricals;" and so, though he accepted the olive-branch at once, it was not in the effusive style in which it was tendered, but rather with an extra assumption of his usual dry manner.

"Of course I forgive you, as you didn't know what you were saying, Bertrand; but it is a mystery to me how all the grief in the world could put such thoughts into your mind —about me, of all men in the world. That I should be your uncle's informant! *I*, of all men!"

"I was mad, I was mad," groaned Bertrand. "Say you are as much my friend as ever."

"Pshaw! let us be done with all this tragedy. There—there's my hand as heartily as ever; and now, for pity's sake, no more of it."

Then they both sat down in silence, Bertrand, with his head bowed down between his hands, plunged in thought. His course lay clear before him, in all save one respect. How was he to break the matter to Eila?—how account for his uncle's stern prohibition, on some ground other than the real one, which she must *never* know?—how make light of the sacrifice she would be sure, in her sensitive mind, to feel that he was making, for her sake, and feel so keenly as perhaps to refuse its acceptance? Pigott, on the other hand, sat comfortably indeed, but motionless as a statue. He, too, was busy in thought, though his face betrayed no emotion. It took him some little time to recover in reality the calmness which he had outwardly affected, and to allay the feelings of chagrin at the outrage which he had himself inflicted on his own stoical theory of action. But that stage being passed, he turned to the consideration of his friend's trouble with a quaint blending of sympathy and worldly *sang froid*.

"What a thing"—so ran his meditations—"what a thing is instinctive antipathy! Now I never liked that girl. I couldn't exactly say why; but I never liked her. Perhaps it was the strain of felonious blood that I detected unconsciously: but then Bertrand didn't detect it; *he* had an instinctive sympathy; odd that,—but then he *is* so odd. He was tremendously fond of her — no doubt of that. Poor Bertrand! That old sweep M'Killop!— any fool could see there was something queer about *him*. *I* always suspected there had been something amiss in *that* quarter; but an actual convict — a *forçat!* Good heavens! fancy my hobnobbing with a *forçat* for three months! But then fancy getting engaged to be married to his daughter! Poor Bertrand! it is awfully hard upon him. Who could have found it out and split to Sir Roland? Some spiteful friend, of course;—some one he had got the better of in a bargain. It's a bad business; but, after all, it's better it came out now. If Bertrand had married her, and found it out afterwards, what would have happened? Illusions can't last for ever. I suppose marriage sends most of them to the right about; and what would he have done? Perhaps defended felony in the abstract, and vowed his own ancestors were robbers and reivers, as all Highland ancestors were: he's capable of any flight; but I suspect—— Well, well, 'many men have died from time to time, and worms, &c.' The fiercest fire, the soonest over. He'll get over it, poor fellow; but it's hard lines for him now—very. I don't think I ever allowed myself to be very sorry for anything before. I suppose *I'll* get over it too; but it's confoundedly disagreeable and painful for me just now.

I had no idea I was so fond of the fellow. Here's the misery and the mistake of indulging the affections. They let you in for all this sort of thing; but I'm not likely to be caught getting fond of another fellow, if I know it;" and his previous refrain of "Poor Bertrand!" was gradually exchanged for "Poor Pigott!"

At last the philosopher spoke.

"Bertrand, old boy."

No answer.

"I say, Bertrand, old fellow, it can do no good to sit moping over the affair; it's dismal enough, in all conscience; I'm sorrier than I ever was before. But, hang it! if the thing's dismal, take some action and be done with it for good and all."

"I *am* going to act," said Bertrand, in a hollow voice; "my mind is quite made up. I am only in doubt about one thing."

"And that is?"

"How to break it to her."

"Oh, my dear fellow, that needn't bother you. Of course you have only to hint delicately that the fact is blown upon, and she'll see the common-sense of the thing; she'll admit the impossibility of the marriage at once.

There will be no fight—that you may depend upon."

"By heavens, Pigott! do you mean—do you dare to mean to hint that she is aware of her father's disgrace?"

"Oh dear, no, no, no—not at all, my dear fellow!" cried Pigott, with unusual alacrity, sorely belying his own convictions, but apprehensive of another scene; "innocent of it as the babe unborn, of course."

"Then what do you mean by 'no fight'?"

"On the part of the *forç*——, of the father, I mean, to be sure."

"And may I just ask what you mean by 'the impossibility of the marriage'?"

"Well, you know, my dear Bertrand, as a man of the world, you must, of course, see that it *is* impossible; there is no blinking *that*, I should say."

"*I* should say, and I *do* say, that I see no impossibility in the matter; exactly the reverse. I'm not a man of the world. God forbid I should be, if being so could make me untrue to her. Marry her I will—that you may depend upon. I would marry her if she were the daughter of Alibaba and the Forty

Thieves, and if I had to take the name and arms of M'Killop into the bargain. Marry her I will."

Pigott was sorely inclined to laugh aloud at the contrast between Bertrand's earnestness and his rather quaint illustrations of it.

"The M'Killop arms," he thought: "now what would the Herald Office give him? On a field sable, a pair of handcuffs proper, perhaps. Crest,—a reputation *coupé* in all its parts. Motto—*Non immemor jugi*—'I can't forget the jug.'"

He preserved his gravity, however, and went on aloud. "Very well, Bertrand, but have you considered everything?"

"I have."

"Your uncle?"

"I disown him."

"Your prospects, then?"

"I sacrifice them."

"But won't you sacrifice hers as well?"

"I can work."

"H'm!—you will write to her, will you, at once?"

"Of course."

"And say—what will you say?"

"I have made up my mind now, I think, about everything. To-night I will write to my uncle, and tell him that I have made my choice, and will cheerfully abide by the results. I will tell him that I have quite decided to accept disinheritance rather than sacrifice both love and honour. He is welcome to do what he pleases with the estate. It would be a miserable inheritance to me with the conditions he wishes to impose; and as for his affection, since I have never perceived it, that part of the disinheritance will not be formidable. When this letter has been posted, *then* I will write to Eila, and tell her that my uncle is cruel and bigoted, and that he forbids our marriage on pain of disinheritance, but that I have gladly accepted this penalty, as I would accept one a thousand-fold severer for her sake."

"Well, Bertrand, if you take my advice you will reverse the order of your letters—you will write first to the lady."

"I won't."

"But in fairness to her; she might think it undesirable to marry a pauper, you know."

"Ah! how little you understand her heart—

her pure, noble character! My reason for not writing to her till *after* I have settled the matter irrevocably by writing to my uncle, is, that I am afraid her over-sensitive regard for me might induce her to decline to let me make the sacrifice—refuse to confirm my disinheritance by any act of hers. She *might* do so; she is immensely disinterested and firm; and so I prefer to put the matter beyond a doubt by my own act, so that she may not even have an opportunity of sacrificing her own love and mine, and the happiness of both, to a regard for my position and prospects."

"Take a night to think of it, old fellow."

"Not an hour—not an instant; I am off to write now. I shall be in a fever till it is done. To-morrow I shall get leave and go down to her. We must look our prospects boldly in the face, and devise some means of overcoming obstacles. When we are together that will be perfectly simple."

And so he left his friend, who sank back in his chair, with a look of much vexation, muttering to himself, "Mad! mad! mad!"

CHAPTER XXIII.

BERTRAND, it may well be supposed, was scarcely in the frame of mind suitable to the composition of a calm letter, and it is not wonderful that his attempt to adopt this tone in his epistle to Sir Roland was on the whole unsuccessful. His first essays—half-a-dozen of them at least—failed to satisfy even his excited mind, as models of the dignified impassibility which he wished to affect, or of the lofty, rebuking, yet despising, tone which seemed appropriate to the occasion.

His first attempt ran thus:—

"Sir Roland Cameron,—

"Burning with a just sense of wrong and outrage, of natural affection mocked, and the heart's best feelings treated as shams and illusions, to be at once dispelled by an application of the test of conventional expediency, I take up my pen to hurl back, with the scorn which it merits, your——"

"No," he thought, "that won't do; it is too wordy. I must be colder, shorter, more incisive;" and he tried again—

"Mr Cameron presents his compliments to Sir Roland Cameron, and, in acknowledging his favour of the —— December, begs to notify to him that he considers that letter as finally dissolving any tie which has heretofore existed between Sir Roland and himself.

"It is obviously superfluous for him to point out to Sir Roland that the tone of that communication is one which, in its pure egotism and dastardly brutality——"

This effort was also torn up in despair, and several others shared the same fate before he achieved the following, which he considered to meet with dignity the requirements of the case:—

"SIR,—Yours of the —— December has

reached me, and my answer to it shall be brief. As it is impossible for me to comply with the injunctions contained in it, and as such compliance is made the condition upon which our present relations are to continue to exist, it is perhaps a waste of time to say more than that I decline the condition, and am prepared to meet the consequences. I will, however, tell you that at the time my engagement was formed, and, in fact, up to the receipt of your letter, I was in ignorance of the painful circumstance to which it alludes. I may even say, farther, that had I been aware of it before my affections and those of the lady were engaged, I should have taken care to avoid contact with her irresistible attractions.

"I can go no further than this, however.

"We are now bound to each other by vows which love and honour alike render sacred; and it appears to me that in accepting disinheritance I make a sacrifice that is very light, when weighed in the balance with the great treasure of her affection. Had it involved the forfeiture of my nearest relative's *affection*, I do not conceal from myself that the sacrifice would have been of a different nature—but *that* it does not involve; and if any proof of this had been necessary (which it was not), your letter would have supplied it, betraying as it does not a mere absence of family affection and sympathy, but a deliberate practical repudiation of the commonest human feeling. I consider it no discredit to be disowned by such a man, in such a cause, but the contrary; and I have the honour to be, your obedient servant,

"BERTRAND CAMERON."

"That, I think, is sufficiently calm and temperate," he exclaimed, as, with hands that trembled with excitement, he folded and addressed the letter. Then, calling his servant, he ordered him to carry it with all speed to the post-office, as if a mail was despatched for the antipodes every five minutes, and he was anxious to catch the very earliest. The paramount business of the evening was thus concluded; he had taken an irrevocable step; he had crossed the river, and blown up the bridge, and in doing so he had taken Eila with him. It was no longer in her power to sacrifice herself to his fortunes; no action of hers could now affect his uncle's conduct. Therefore she was his irrevocably—a reflection that went far to soothe the tumult and trouble of his mind.

Another duty, however, remained to him— he must write to Eila; and long and anxiously did he debate with himself as to the line he should take in addressing her.

Of course she must be carefully guarded from any knowledge of her father's disgrace. The strong measures which his uncle proposed to take, and would now inevitably carry out, required, however, to be accounted for by some strong motive; and what should he say? What adequate motive could be assigned? A determined resolve that his heir should make an ambitious match? Jealousy of any such step initiated without his counsel and advice? An autocratic temper? A contradictory disposition? Was any one of these sufficient to account for so uncompromising a veto? It was very puzzling to him, and the more he tried to convey on paper a clear impression of the absoluteness of the veto, and, at the same time, a vague and general idea of the reasons for it, the more hopeless the task appeared; and he resolved finally to trust to finding at a personal interview the means of expressing what he wished to express, and of suppressing what it was necessary to suppress, and in the mean time merely to state, in a general way, that his uncle was thoroughly unpropitious. And so he wrote as follows :—

"DEAREST EILA,—I have just received my uncle's answer; and though I knew that he was a hard and obstinate man, I was not prepared to find him violently opposed to our union, which, I grieve to say, his letter shows him to be. I need not say, however, that no obstacle, in that or any other quarter, can in the slightest degree affect my resolution; and as I know that your love cannot be altered by the fear or the necessity of sacrifice and hardship, I am perfectly cheerful, and all the more so that it is necessary I should go down to Scotland at once, that I may see you, and consult with you as to our immediate plans and prospects. I shall leave London to-morrow night, and be with you on the following forenoon. In looking forward to this, I lose the sense of all earthly troubles. Oh! my beloved—

. . . . .

. . . . .

Thine own for ever,
"BERTRAND CAMERON."

We prefer to leave the latter part of this letter in the skeleton form, and we think that no enlightened reader will consider that the step requires an apology.

The next morning early—very early for him—Pigott came to his friend's quarters, and found him already up and dressed. The troubles of yesterday had left their marks on his face and on his manner; the former was grave and fixed in its expression, and the latter very calm, quiet, and uniform — somewhat pathetically bereft of its impetuous and cheery characteristics.

"Well, Bertrand," cried Pigott, plunging at once into the subject which had been uppermost in the thoughts of both since they had met—"well, did you write any letters last night?"

"Yes, I did; two letters."

"What! not to your uncle?"

"Yes; one was to Sir Roland Cameron."

"And saying what you said yesterday afternoon that you would say?"

"Precisely."

"You couldn't be such a—— I mean, you didn't post it, I trust?"

"On the contrary, it was posted five minutes after it was sealed up."

"What madness! I never—even I, cool as I am—wrote an important letter overnight, without finding that it required a great deal of alteration in the morning."

"If I had reflected for a century, I could not have altered a syllable I wrote, except perhaps to make it stronger. It is quite useless our discussing the matter, Pigott. The letter is beyond recall, even if I wished—which I don't—to recall it."

"Talking of a century, the only consolation I can see in the whole affair is, that it will be all the same a hundred years hence."

"I don't admit that. In the history of human sorrow and happiness, one page will read differently."

"Who are to be the readers?—But I meant as to yourself."

"That opens a wide question. Are you a materialist?"

"That opens another wide question. Do you believe in the Elysian fields, and that, the course of true love running smooth on this side Styx, you are going to twine garlands of amaranth for Miss Eila to all eternity?"

"I am not at all in the humour for joking."

"Poor old boy! I beg your pardon; your lines are very hard; but you have sadly blundered. To temporise, to resist passively—anything but a declaration of war—was your policy."

"Quite impossible; Eila means Life to me."

"Oh! then I have nothing more to say," said Pigott hastily, shrinking, with all his concern for his friend, from another repetition of the oft-told tale of his love. "But as to the immediate present, what are your plans?"

"I am just now going to the Colonel to ask him for leave to go down to Edinburgh tonight, and to get me a fortnight from the General."

"Are the M'Killops still in Edinburgh?"

"Yes."

"But what are you going to propose, to do, when you get there?"

"First, I shall have to explain how matters stand to Eila, and then we shall have to consider as to our future. The chances are, Mr M'Killop will withdraw his consent, and then I shall have to run off with her, and I must get something to do."

"What! leave the old regiment?"

"I am very sorry to leave the old regiment, but as staying in it means pauperism, there is no help for it."

"But what *can* you do?"

"That is the question one always asks a discharged soldier when he comes to invite one to help him to a situation, and he never has an answer; no more have I, at present."

"Well, I generally find the old soldier has an impression that he could 'keep a gate;' it seems to be the veteran's dream of the *summum bonum*—perhaps equivalent to the retiring officer's idea that he could be an adjutant of volunteers."

"Well, something of that sort might turn up."

"Oh! that would never suit you."

"Something else, then, may turn up; but beggars have no right to a choice. I have no time now, though, to discuss such things; I must go and catch the Colonel: I shall see you afterwards. I go to town by the four o'clock train, if I get leave."

The Colonel made no difficulty about leave, but he was unfortunately absent from his quarters when Bertrand first called, and did not return in time to admit of his catching the night-train from London—a sore trial to the impetuous lover, for which, however, there was no remedy. So, after a *tête-à-tête* dinner with Pigott—a meal conducted in silence (for Bertrand was deeply preoccupied, and Pigott felt that his friend had run himself into a *cul-de-sac*, from which no wit or wisdom of his could devise an exit), he departed for London, slept there, and next morning started for Edinburgh.

CHAPTER XXIV.

THE northern mail did not behave in a satisfactory way. Freighted with such a Jonah as an impatient lover, it was sure to lose time; and it did so. The rails were "sticky," it was alleged; there was an unusual rush of passengers at every station where a stoppage was made, so that fresh carriages had to be constantly attached; and every *employé* seemed, in Bertrand's eyes, to go about his business with unparalleled languor and apathy. "Shall I be in time to see her to-night?" was the constant refrain of his thoughts. The delay at York was so intolerable that he felt certain the refreshment people and the conductors of the train must be in collusion. "Five-and-forty minutes behind already!" he remarked, bitterly, to the guard, as he banged the door shut before starting from the latter station; " how much more time do you mean to lose?"

"As little as possible, sir," said the official; "but we shall be late to-night: great run on the trains these last two days. We'll do our best though, for *you*, sir," he added, confidentially, introducing the upper half of his body at the window, and giving a suggestive prominence to his right hand.

"Ten shillings if we lose no more time, and another ten if we pick up what we've lost," said Bertrand.

"Thankee, sir; I'll speak to the driver."

"Here, g-guard," added a new and now the sole other occupant of the carriage, "I'll st-and something too. I'm in a hi-hurry to ge-get to Ed-ed-ed-ed——"

"Edinburgh," supplemented Bertrand, in a fever of impatience, adding, "I beg your pardon, but we're losing time."

"D-don't me-mention it. You shall have te-ten bob, guard, on the same terms."

"All right, sir—whew!" and off went the train. The new arrival was a young and gorgeous being, clothed in purple and fine linen —that is, with every sort of embellishment belonging to the very height of the fashion. "Astracan fur" was the first idea suggested by his appearance, and then "the gold of Ophir," these two materials being prominent features in his array; but, investigated in detail, his equipments furnished the eye and the mind with a hundred glorious points on which they might rest in wonder, if not in delight. The massive rings encrusting his fingers were worthy of a Begum; his boots, from their radiance, might have been mirrors for Beau Brummel; his morocco dressing-case, delicate in tint and exquisitely mounted, was a casket worthy of crown jewels; and his cigar-case, splendid with gold and blue velvet, a fitting receptacle for the cigarettes of a sultana. About all this bloom and flash a subtle aroma of fragrant essences ambrosially hovered. But if art had done much for this gentleman, nature had bestowed her favours on him with a niggard hand; the face which surmounted all this magnificence was almost pathetically in contrast to it. Nothing could well be less attractive. It failed in colour, as well as in contour and expression; being in all these respects vividly suggestive of the mealy side of a halfpenny roll—pale, fat, flabby, and vacant. Its only relief was a little yellow sprouting on the upper lip, evidently much believed in as a moustache by the rest of the body, for it was incessantly caressed by the gemmy fingers, and the upper lip lifted it up proudly now and then, for the inspection of the ferrety eyes.

"I really beg your pardon," said Bertrand, politely, when the train was in motion; "my impatience quite made me forget my manners."

"N-n-not a bit of it. Every one used to chi-chi-chaff me about my ist-tammering. I don't mind it now; it's n-n-n-othing now. You sh—ould—have heard me before I was kick-kick-kick-kick-cured!"

"Was it so very bad then?" asked Bertrand, gravely.

"Pi-pawsitively he-eathenish."

"Indeed!" said Bertrand, thinking that, viewed as a test of orthodoxy, his companion's present utterance would not bring him far within the pale.

"And, pray, how did they cure you?"

"They gave me dr-ops."

"What kind of drops?"

"D-don't know; d-rops, and dee-evilish nasty dr-ops too."

Hereupon he lighted a gigantic cabana,

opened his travelling-bag, took out 'Punch,' cut the pages with a splendid paper-knife, looked at a picture, and then laid it aside.

'The Field' underwent a similar process, but it also failed to excite his literary appetite, and he returned to conversation.

"You're in the army?"

"Yes, I am; how do you know?"

"Lo-ook like it; infantry, though."

"Why?"

"Oh! I know the lo-ook of a man in the if-feet."

"Well, I *am* in infantry, and I'm glad of it."

"RE-EALLY! I'm in kick-cavalry—the —th; I'm kick-Coppinger of the —th Hoo-sars; in the regiment they call me 'the Kicker'—ki-cursed if I know why. What is your regiment?"

"The —th; I'm Cameron of the —th."

"Don't know 'em. Of course you're on your way to our ib-ib-ball?"

"Ball? no; where is it to be?"

"Edinburgh, of course. Don't you know about it, and the hard le-lines we've had?"

Bertrand confessed his ignorance of the ball

and of any special grief lately arrived to the gallant —th; whereupon Mr Coppinger explained that the —th had been quartered at Edinburgh for the last year, and had not expected to be moved thence for another month; on the faith of which, they had issued invitations, and made all the preparations for a grand ball, when a sudden order had arrived for their removal to York. They had determined, however, not to give up the ball; and though half the regiment was in York, and half on the march, most of the officers would turn up that night, to do the honours in Edinburgh.

"Pill-ucky, aint it?"

"Very plucky, indeed."

"Why aint you coming?"

"Because I'm not asked, for one thing."

"Never mind; I'll give you a ticket."

"You're very good, indeed; but I'm going down on business, and have to see people to-night."

"You ought to come. We're going to take the shi-ne out of everything: Fif-rancatelli's ki-cock swell is down; you'd better come, just to see how the old —th come to the fif-ront."

"I've no doubt it will be magnificent, but I fear I can't come."

"L-ots of jolly people going, and no end of pip-retty girls. They're tre-mendous nuts on us there. They ki-call us the handsome hoosars, you know."

"I suppose you're a good-looking lot."

"We are—we are; that's j-ust where it is;—no plain heads among *us*."

After this the Kicker fell asleep, and Bertrand was left to his meditations, and his ever-increasing impatience; for they did not make up lost time, but lost more and more; so that, time and the hour at last working their way, when the train rumbled into the Waverley Station at Edinburgh it was very long overdue.

"Going to dine?" inquired Mr Coppinger of Bertrand when they had arrived at the hotel where they had both decided to put up.

"No, I can't eat; I shall just change a little and go out."

"And you won't do the ball?"

"No—many thanks."

"I don't think I'll dine either: a br-andy-and-soda, and then wait for Fif-rancatelli;

that's about my shape, I be-lieve. Now I must go and dress. Good-night."

" Good-night."

And they separated.

Bertrand made all haste with his toilette arrangements, but it was already well on to eleven o'clock when he turned into George Street, where was the M'Killops' hotel.

All along that street, and in the side streets running into it, strings of carriages were slowly creeping up to the Assembly Rooms, from the opened windows of which strains of bright dance-music were already floating, telling that the revels of the " handsome hussars" had begun.

" It must be late, but they can't have gone to bed yet. Eila would expect me to-night, although I failed in the morning," thought Bertrand, as, with a palpitating heart, he rang the bell at the hotel.

" Mrs M'Killop at home ?"

" Gone out half an hour ago, sir."

" Out ?—to a party ?"

" To the ball, sir—the officers' ball."

" And Mr M'Killop ?"

" Gone too, sir."

"Luck!" thought Bertrand. "I shall have a *tête-à-tête*. Well, no matter," he continued; "say to Miss M'Killop that Mr Cameron is here, and would be glad to see her, if he may."

"But Miss M'Killop has gone too, sir."

"To the ball?" cried Bertrand, in such a tone of surprise that the man looked astonished in his turn.

"Yes, sir, to the ball."

"I will call to-morrow morning, then," said Bertrand, and abruptly turned away.

Eila gone to the ball! to any ball! it was almost inconceivable. Could he have mistaken the man? No; his words had been perfectly clear. Eila gone to the ball! And as if in a dream, he walked away in the opposite direction from the Rooms, without knowing or heeding where he went. It was not in accordance with the old-world theory that a *fiancée*, from the moment of her betrothal, should abandon all festive scenes, that he felt overcome with painful surprise on learning that his betrothed was where she was; but it was the contrast between what she was doing and what he understood her feelings to be, that so affected him.

Could *he* have gone to a ball without her?

Could he have mixed in such a scene, with its mock devotions and airy gallantries—he to whom the idea of all other women was indifferent, if not distasteful? he whose heart was entirely filled and engrossed with the one object of his love?

And did not she feel as he did? Eila at a ball! It was inconceivable.

At such a time too! at such a crisis in their fate!

It was true that she did not know how grave the crisis was; but she *did* know that formidable difficulties had presented themselves. And then, he thought, how cruelly out of keeping with the real state of the case—with his disinheritance—with the sadness, the humiliation, the perplexities that surrounded them—with his own sorrowful emotions of the last two days—was the atmosphere of a ball-room. He said to himself that Eila's conduct was cruel,—inexplicable, at least, and, until explained, provisionally to be considered cruel. Long and sadly, up and down the now emptied streets, poor Bertrand wandered, consumed with all sorts of miserable feelings, disappointment, weariness of spirit, heart-sickness, and jealousy; for it is not to be supposed that the green-eyed monster did not suggest, " Can she have had any *special* inducement?"

Up and down he wandered, and, every now and then, there came to him in his desolation, from the gay scene where she, no doubt, was the cynosure of eyes, a wandering wave of voluptuous music, quickening the disquiet of his thoughts. But Bertrand's love was obstinately loyal, and manfully fought Eila's battle for her.

And so, by degrees, extenuating circumstances were discerned, and then not long after, came her complete acquittal. She was unhappy, he thought, and depressed—deeply disappointed at his non-arrival; in this state, importuned, perhaps, to go by her step-mother, she had not had the energy to contend with that energetic person.

Or perhaps (and what more likely?) she had gone, in the hope that, when he arrived, he would follow her thither. What more likely than that, as a soldier, he should be invited, and going to, a military ball?

Yes, that must have been it; poor dear

Eila! she had been thoughtless — nothing more; indeed it could scarcely be called thoughtless of her; in point of fact, it could *not* be called thoughtless. And how cruelly and harshly he had been thinking of her!

With these mollified feelings came an irrepressible desire to see her that night—at once—on the very instant.

"Fancy my being within a few hundred yards of her for two hours, without rushing to see her!" he exclaimed; "I must be mad. I will go to this ball at once; she shall not be disappointed—my angel!" Then he reflected on the lateness of the hour; the ball would be half over; and then his dress had to be changed. Nevertheless, he must see her somehow; and so, without any definite plan of proceeding, he turned in the direction of the Assembly Rooms.

Arrived at the entrance corridor, he found it all ablaze with the splendours which pertain to the balls of the military—trophies of arms, fantastic dispositions of light, flowers, evergreens, banners, insignia. A guard of honour of the regiment lounged sleepily (for arrivals had, of course, long since ceased) along the entire length of the passage; and up the centre Bertrand walked mechanically. The chances are he might have walked up-stairs and into the ball-room with his hat on, so deep was his preoccupation, had he not been observed and swooped upon by a sergeant who was fulfilling the duties of watch-dog.

"Ticket, sir! ticket!" said Cerberus, letting his eye fall at a depreciating angle upon Bertrand's morning dress.

"Ticket? oh, I forgot;—ticket? to be sure; I haven't got one; but send up to Mr Coppinger, and say a gentleman wishes to speak to him for a moment."

After a short delay Mr Coppinger came cackling and jingling down in full panoply.

"Ki-couldn't make it out," he said. "L-arkins swore you must be a b-ailiff. Larkins thinks of nothing else—small blame to him. Tre-mendously glad you've ki-come; but, I say!" suddenly glancing at Bertrand's costume, "these o-veralls and boots, you know! ki-couldn't dance so, eh?"

"No, no," said Bertrand; "the fact is, I didn't feel sleepy, and I thought I would come and merely have a look at the ball, somehow, if possible. I knew it would be splendid; so if you can stow me away somewhere—at the back of the orchestra, or anywhere, I shall be much obliged."

"Wo-on't it be slow, though?"

"Not a bit."

"Well, I'll put you in the gi-gallery, in the sc-second room, where our band plays—best room—all round d-ances there—and you can s-see them supping. Gi-gallery's fi-full of maids, though. Do you mind?"

"Not a bit."

"After the people are gone you can come down and s-s-sup; and I'll bring you s-something to dr-ink after next dance."

"You are awfully good."

And so the good-natured fellow installed Bertrand in the gallery, and went away to fulfil his duty as a "handsome hussar."

CHAPTER XXV.

THE gallery which faced the orchestra was, in the second assembly room thrown open on such great occasions, to supplement the dancing space of the first. It was, as the Kicker had said, filled with servants, principally of the fair sex, who seemed to sit there through the long hours, patient and pleased; perhaps on the principle which rivets the street-boy's nose to the cook-shop's window, or spell-bound by that mysterious fascination which the contemplation of dress exercises on the minds of all womankind.

The ball was at its height when Bertrand took his seat. The bandsmen of the gallant —th, with purple cheeks and staring eyeballs, were testing to the uttermost the strength of their very brazen instruments, incited by a foreign bandmaster, whose ecstatic gesticulations suggested the "finish" of a flat race.

Down below, in the hall, there was a whirling, indistinguishable circle of bright colours—scarlet, gold, blue, green, silver, pink, mauve—all the colours of the rainbow,—casting out, every now and then, from its circumference, some couple whom fatigue or dilapidation had compelled to succumb; and these figures, panting on the brink, were the only sort of key to the composition of the great *zoetrope* they had left. On either side of the room, a portion was screened off with light partitions of calico and muslin; there were the supper-tables, and there there was no less earnest application to the business of the moment.

For the hour of the chaperone and of the heavy father had come; their sturdy phalanx assailed the works of Francatelli with a deadly impact, and between their intervals strenuously skirmished that furtive cloud of *guerilleros*, whose evening campaign opens with the supper-room, and closes when the last light is turned out, or the last bottle has been emptied. The room was a blaze of light, the atmosphere was loaded with the breath of exotic flowers and shrubs, heated as in a forcing-house for tropical plants, and vibrating with the hurly-burly of a general action. Bertrand, coming into this scene from the quiet dark street and his own dark thoughts, felt stupefied, and almost giddy. There was no rest for the eye—all was motion and whirl everywhere, down to the minutest details,—from the sweep of the conductor's *baton* to the flashing knives and forks and teeth behind the screens. His first thought was, that he should never see Eila there, that even love's keen vision would fail to recognise its object in that eddying throng; and so indeed it might have been, if the bandsman of the —th had only been endowed with the Homeric throat and lungs of adamant; for the *zoetrope* was continually recruited by new arrivals from the other room, and from behind the screens.

But a cavalry bandsman—even when inspired with the "orgiastic rage" of a regimental ball, and goaded on by an Italian maniac—is, after all, mere flesh and blood; and at last, after achieving a climax of unparalleled noise and pace, the protracted galop came to an abrupt close, as though a well-earned apoplexy had suddenly arrested the musicians. Then the circle resolved itself into its elements. Streams of exhausted dancers, flowed, breathless and dishevelled, in all directions,—to the supper-tables—to the sequestered bowers of flirtation which an advanced civilisation has added to the seductions of the place —to the principal room, where, on an awful dais, the chaperones—the field-marshals and generals, as it were, of the action—watched the tide of battle, and devised strategic combinations. In less than half a minute the floor was empty, and all the life which Bertrand had now to watch was clustered about the supper-tables. In vain he scanned every group, in vain he overhauled every new entrance; they gave him no more satisfaction than when they were all whirling round together, blended in the kaleidoscopic circle of the dance; for Eila was nowhere to be seen. In vain, too, did he look for her father and Mrs M'Killop—so pre-eminently, he should have thought, and indeed knew to be, of the supper-loving class. What had become of them all? Perhaps they had gone; perhaps they had no acquaintances to bring them to this room; perhaps Eila had no partners. The idea of Eila having no partners! After all, the idea was not insupportable to him; but then, he might sit there all night among the patient handmaidens, for nothing.

Here his meditations were broken in upon by a voice from behind. "Can't you let a fi-fellow pass?" and, looking round, he saw the benevolent Coppinger shoving through the crowd towards him, followed by a servant bearing a bottle of champagne and a tumbler.

"Br-ought you something to wet your whistle with," he said; "st-unning ball, aint it? did you see me with that girl in blue? pace and fi-form, wasn't it?"

"It was magnificent," said Bertrand; "but I am ashamed to drink, all by myself, here—in this public place."

"Ash-amed! I would be ashamed to refuse this liquor in a ca-thedral. Ti-toss it off;" and Bertrand tossed it off,—some four hundred thirsty eyes supervising the process.

"I must be off now," said Coppinger; "I'm engaged, and it don't do to throw over, at one's own ball. Besides, the pi-party is out of the common. Just you watch while I bring her in. I've r-re-gularly brought her out, you know. I dis-ki-covered her. I danced with her — ne-nine times last week; and people notice it. I've made her fi-fortune. She's aw-fully pip-retty, and ho-o-orribly spi-pooney upon me."

"Indeed! what is her name?"

"Don't re-member; life is too short to re-member S-ki-cotch names." And the Kicker went away, and left Bertrand again to himself.

By degrees the supper-tables grew emptier; the bandsmen returned to their places; and stray couples began to enter and walk round the arena, waiting for the next dance.

Suddenly it seemed to Bertrand that all the lights in the room gave a spasmodic start. Floor, walls, and ceiling seemed to turn round; and over everything a sort of mist or dimness spread itself — over everything save on one spot in the centre of the area below, where, in the full lustre of her beauty, stood Eila—Eila at last—more beautiful than he had ever seen her look before, every charm enhanced by the perfect taste of her toilette, her lovely face lighted up by the excitement of the occasion, and by conscious triumph. Different, truly, from the Eila he had expected to meet, who was to have received him, of course, with joy —but a joy that could only be called forth by his advent—a joy that was to rise before his very eyes, suddenly, from clouds of depression and anxiety. His original astonishment at finding she had gone to the ball was nothing to his bewilderment now; bewilderment is the only word to express his feelings. Two trains of thought seemed to flow concurrently in his mind,—one devoted entirely to Eila herself, to her presence, to her beauty, to herself, his goddess, his idol; the other to his own misery at finding her there, bright, radiant, happy, without a shadow of a shade of abstraction from the sparkling scene of the moment. Gazing at her in his bewilderment, a sort of wonder came over him that *she* should not see *him*—that his concentration upon her should not draw her eyes to him by some magnetic sympathy. Attracted thus to observe minutely the object of her attention, his eye fell upon a vague shadow beside her— a thing which had appeared to move itself and to gesticulate, but which he had associated with nothing and nobody, till now, as he looked curiously at it, the full sunbeam of Eila's smile fell upon it, and revealed Mr Coppinger.

She, then, was this fellow's *protégée!*—the girl whose fortune he was making—who was in love with him!—the loathsome brute! Something much less subtle than a magnetic attraction all but drew him down to the area below. Luckily for Mr Coppinger, he mastered the impulse for the moment; and a moment after, the music striking up, the dance began, and he had the satisfaction of seeing the hussar encircle Eila's waist with one arm, while, with an airy wave of the other, and a smile of ineffable sweetness (responded to by his partner), he led her to the brink of the vortex, and plunged in. Somebody else's arm round Eila's waist was bad enough—but that somebody else, a vapouring, chattering imbecile, who patronised *her*—*his* Eila—who affected to be trifling with her feelings—who trumpeted about to all the world that this girl loved him to distraction—hopelessly too—with the passion of some miserable little *bourgeoise*, madly centred upon a grand seigneur!

And then her smiles—her smiles of encouragement to this creature—this object! All this was too overwhelming for mere wrath: it was simply paralysing. Read by the light of this new revelation, he began to doubt his own identity, and that of Eila;—everything became unreal to him. The dance went on and ended, and he sat staring stupidly at the scene below, noting, now without any special astonishment, that as Eila took her seat on one of the benches, she was the object of her partner's tenderest attention. He stared woodenly at Coppinger's attitude of confidential *empressement*. He saw him take Eila's bouquet from her hand, and, after an interrogative gesture, select a flower from it; —he saw her suggest another flower with her most bewitching smile, and actually give it to the wretch;—he saw all this, quite paralysed out of the power of surprise or wrath. Others soon came—other demons in uniform—in one sense worse than the first, for they were comely, shapely demons; and about her there was a cloud of candidates for partnership, Coppinger's face twisted into a leer of confidential meaning, seeming to suggest, "Throw 'em over, stick to me—to Coppinger, whom you adore."

One after another bore her off, but brought her back — always back — to the same seat, whence the fishy eyes of the Kicker had followed her, with an expression of proprietorship. Where *was* Mrs M'Killop? and why did Eila not go to *her*? It was but a passing ripple of curiosity; nothing could surprise him now.

So the band trumpeted, and the dancers danced, and the suppers supped, and Coppinger leered, and Eila flirted, and Bertrand still sat staring on. At last the room began to grow emptier; to grow very empty; through the few little windows in the roof daylight began to peer; the noise about the supper-tables grew uproarious; and the subtle odour of cigars began to steal into the hall—all symptoms that the revel was drawing to a close, and the guests departing.

All unheeded by Bertrand, who sat in a state of *coma*, almost alone now, in his pride of place, where he might have been sitting to this hour if the stalwart figure of Mrs M'Killop had not at last flaunted into the room, and hurriedly approached her step-daughter.

Mrs M'Killop was shawled, and her gesticulations were those of haste. Eila rose; Coppinger appeared to make an attempt to dissuade Mrs M'Killop from her departure; but that proving futile, he gave Eila his arm, and the party left the room. Then Bertrand's spell was broken, and he sprang from his seat and followed them. At the foot of the stair, the first person he saw was Coppinger waiting at the door of the cloak-room.

"Here you are!" cried the unconscious hussar; "supper, now — Fi-francatelli, and no mistake about it!"

"I have had enough," said Bertrand.

"Did Jennings take you up some more? Holloa! you look a little fi-flustered; but you'll have no head in the morn-ing; you can trust our liquor; that's just where it is, you know."

"I want nothing more," said Bertrand, his eye and his mind fastened on the cloak-room.

"Ah! you've been bi-bored, I see. Well, you know, if you had changed your things you might have danced. Don't bl-ame me."

"I don't."

"I say, did you see me with her? She gave me this flower. She's awfully spi-pooney tonight; doosed near pip-prop-posed, I expect; Larkins says that giving this flower meant a pi-pop; but I'm too old a bird to be ki-caught by——"

The declaration was, however, interrupted, for here Eila appeared at the doorway. Her eye fell at once upon Bertrand; she gave a vivid start, then instantly rushed forward with outstretched hands. "What! Bertrand? What a surpr— No, I don't mean that, for I knew you would come; indeed, I *felt* you were here. But why so late? why didn't you come sooner, and dance with me?"

"I have been here half the night, and I have *seen* you—I have had *that* satisfaction, at all events," he said, in a significant tone; and here Mrs M'Killop came forth with another *protégée*; and after expressions of surprise, welcome, and so forth, she took the arm of an old gentleman who was waiting for her, and wishing Bertrand "Good-night," and telling the young ladies to follow her, turned to depart.

Whereupon Coppinger presented his arm to Eila, who drew back, however.

"Why, you said I might," exclaimed the Kicker.

"Yes, Mr Coppinger, but I'm sorry you can't; Mr Cameron is to take me down—if he will, that is," she added, with an imploring look at her lover's dark countenance.

"I came for the purpose," said Bertrand, grimly; and Coppinger muttering something about "doosed bad fi-form" and "the fi-feet all over," gave his arm to the other young lady, and went down-stairs.

"My darling! What joy! I am alive again!" said Eila, as she took Bertrand's arm.

"You seemed pretty lively all the evening," said Bertrand, shortly.

"Did I? yet I was miserable. I *felt* you were somewhere in the hall. I knew you could see me, though I couldn't see you; and that was cruel—that made me wretched. But I said to myself, 'I'll choose the ugliest man in the room to dance with, and not make Bertrand jealous;' and I did, didn't I, dear?"

"You did, certainly."

"And when I gave the creature that flower, I thought, 'Now Bertrand is having a hearty laugh.' Did you see it?"

"I did."

"And did you laugh quite loud out?"

"Not quite."

"Why, Bertrand, you ridiculous, cross, old fellow! Is it possible? No, no, it can't be; you can't have been jealous of such a creature as that?"

"Jealous?" said Bertrand, beginning to feel a little ashamed of himself. "N-no; the fact is, I—I didn't expect you to be at the ball."

"And you came here to amuse yourself, without coming to see poor me! when I've been so miserable, and watching at the window all day, and crying—crying, and so unhappy; and you so unfeel-eel-ing." And she began to sob.

"Hush, Eila! hush, my own darling! People are looking."

"I don't care—who looks. You don't care —for my love. You throw it back to me, although you pretended to wish—to have it— so much; and I had been counting the hours —till you came; and now you are come, you are—all changed—and hate me; and I wish I was dead; and I only went to please mamma; and because you might have dressed and followed, if you had cared for me, instead of coming like a pol-ol-iceman, spying, and cross, and cruel."

"Be calm, my darling Eila!" whispered Bertrand, secretly delighted with this ebullition, but some remorse mingling with his joy; "be calm. Of course I went to your hotel first, and followed on in the hope of getting a glimpse of you; and I did; and somehow I didn't like to see you with all these fellows hanging about you. I couldn't help it, you know;—and I thought you were looking so happy, and——"

"Happy! oh, Bertrand!" (in the dismalest of minors.)

"Well, perhaps not happy, but cheery," amended Bertrand : "and I know—well, no, I don't know—what it was, but I was unhappy, and miserable, and mad. I suppose it's human nature."

"And you love poor me the same as ever, darling Bertrand?"

"I adore you;—and you?"

"I worship you."

"Angel!"

"Beloved!"

"And they looked into each other's eyes, and neither saw ought but truth in those mysterious and mystifying orbs.

"When can I see you to-morrow, Eila?"

"Whenever you please, dear Bertrand!"

"You will be tired; you must rest, after all this fatigue; and I have a great deal to say to you—something that will agitate you, perhaps; and I should like to have a long talk with you before I see the others."

"You frighten me, dearest! what is it?"

"Don't be frightened; there is nothing alarming," said Bertrand, with a laugh; "but suppose we go out together—to some quiet place, where we can talk without being interrupted."

"Very well; call for me."

"At twelve o'clock?"

"Yes, that will do. Good-night. Dream of me; and oh, darling, love me always!"

"For ever! Good-night."

As Bertrand gazed after the carriage, lost in sweet thoughts, a voice broke upon his ear vaguely, like the far-off hum of insects—

"Confounded ch-eek of yours, taking that g-irl away from me! spoiling spi-port, too! What are you? A ki-cousin? or what?"

"Dream of me; and oh, darling, love me

always!" murmured Bertrand, in a voice of rapt abstraction.

"I'll be d-d-dashed if I do!" replied the literal Kicker. "You've treated me ski-candalously;" and he confronted Bertrand with a look of vinous ferocity.

"Oh!" said Bertrand, waking up and looking at the hussar. "Oh yes, I recollect now; you wanted to take Miss M'Killop to her carriage?"

"Of course I did."

"Well, she preferred going with me. It wasn't my fault. I'm sorry she showed such bad taste. Is there anything more to be said?"

"L-ots more! s-atisfaction; wait here till I consult Larkins."

"That I certainly can't; but you and Larkins can bring the result of your consultation to me in the morning. Good-night," and he walked away.

"I dec-ec-line to say goo-goo-goo——" but Bertrand was out of ear-shot before the angry sentence was completed. What to him was the wrath of all the hussars in Christendom, inspired as he was, at the moment? and what to him, now, all grief, pain, doubts, misgivings, and obstacles? They faded as nocturnal visions fade before the sun, and vanished from the shining circle which Love's light cast around him.

CHAPTER XXVI.

THE next morning, Bertrand, of whose offence Larkins had probably taken a lenient view (for Mr Coppinger made no sign), kept tryst punctually, and found Eila waiting for him ready to go out. She was alone; Mrs M'Killop was still sleeping off the dissipation of the ball, and Mr M'Killop had gone out on business.

"You look pale and tired, Eila," said Bertrand; "perhaps we had better not walk: shall we be private here?"

"Yes, but let us go out. Now I am with you, I shan't be pale and tired any more; and besides, the open air will do me good. Let us go to the Gardens."

The meeting of two lovers in the gardens of a city street does not suggest the Arcadian simplicity or the picturesque *entourage* with which poets love to associate such occasions;

but those who know the gardens fronting Princes Street in Edinburgh, will scarcely object to them on æsthetic grounds in such a connection, lying as they do in a situation at once unique and beautiful. Urban life indeed (though of a chastened, uncommercial character) lies on one side, but on the other the great Castle Rock—weird and rugged—rears itself abruptly from the verdant lawns that lie at its feet, and cast far up to the ledges and slopes on its precipitous side, embracing arms of foliage, and countless tributes of clustering wildflowers—the attitude, as it were, and the offerings of humble love.

Hither came the lovers, and following instinctively a secluded path that wound round the westward face of the rock, arrived at a shady seat high up upon the slope; and there, sitting themselves down, Bertrand essayed to open his momentous subject. It was difficult, though. Eila had evidently formed no conception of the real nature of the crisis. Not a word, indeed, had escaped either of them on the subject, but her manner showed that she had not interpreted his letter in an alarming sense, probably imagining that nothing farther was amiss than the angry surprise of a churlish old uncle at finding his nephew had formed an early engagement without special advantages. Bertrand's letter might have conveyed more to a stranger, but Eila understood his various phases, and knew that with him there might be tragical language where there was nothing that the world at large would have considered tragedy. Bertrand found the task difficult, therefore, and painful, and he shrank from inflicting on Eila the grief and agitation which he knew his words must bring; and so, with all his anxiety to commence, with all his concentration on the subject, he fell into the mere human track of stalking it, as it were, and started off on all sorts of trivial subjects, which had no conceivable bearing on the matter in hand. In this way he drew Eila's attention, at considerable length, to the exquisite lights and shadows lying on the distant hills of Fife, to the smoke of steamers in the Firth, to the flight of sea-birds, to the mathematical precision of the street parallels below, finally to a solitary goat standing contemplatively on a little ledge above them. On this animal he descanted philosophically, artistically, zoologically, and historically, diverging from the goat to the ibex, one of which species he had shot on a *precisely* similar ledge in Spain, some years ago, which reminded him of a quaint anecdote, and, and, &c.—and so he went on "meandering." Even the usual half baby-talk of lovers was barred to him, for that would have at once brought him up to the subject he wished to reach, and was doing his best to avoid.

Eila, accustomed to his wild and fervid declarations and demonstrations of love, found all this a little tame by comparison, and besides, she wished to hear "the news;" so, after her interest had flagged dismally, which was made apparent by yawning and other symptoms, she abruptly opened the subject herself by saying—

"Well, dear Bertrand, you've told me nothing of your news. Is the terrible uncle very angry?"

"Yes, Eila, he is very angry."

"What a cross old thing! Why is he very angry?"

"He disapproves of our engagement."

"Of any engagement of yours, or of this especially?"

"Both, in a way."

"He objects to poor me?"

"He has never seen you, you know, my darling."

"Have you got his letter here?"

"No, I have not."

"Why not?"

"It made me so angry. It would have done no good to bring it."

"And what do you think of it all?"

"I love you more than ever."

"Yes, but I mean——"

"I love you with a devotion that is only increased by obstacles, with a——"

"Yes, yes, but tell me——"

"With an ecstatic——"

"I know you do, my dearest Bertrand; but speak of your uncle. If he thinks in this way, what are we to do?"

"Get married."

"But if he is so violently opposed?"

"Get married."

"Ah, he doesn't actually forbid it, then?"

"Yes, he does."

"But if we get married, you mean that he will get over his anger and be pacified in time? and I am sure I could coax and persuade him. I might write him a charming little humble letter, and enclose him my photograph —the coloured one, you know. I am certain I could pacify him."

"I think you could do anything else but that."

"He won't be pacified?"

"Nothing short of a miracle would do that."

"Ah, you don't know my powers. Let me try."

"But you don't mind his prohibition, do you?"

"Yes, I do mind it very much. It is dreadfully wicked to disobey one's parents and guardians; the Bible says so."

"I know; but if a wicked parent or a wicked guardian wantonly gives a wicked order?"

"Is your uncle wicked, then?"

"He is——no, I won't say what he is; but I should not be doing wrong in disobeying this order of his."

"Darling Bertrand, I don't know whether it is right or wrong. I'm afraid I am dreadfully reckless and wicked. I'm afraid I don't really care about anything now, or think of anything, but you."

"And you will marry me in spite of everything?"

"Can you ask me? I am yours for ever and ever."

A blank here occurred in the conversation, which the reader can fill in according to his idea of probabilities. Bertrand closed the hiatus by resuming—

"And you fear no privations — no hardships?"

"With you I should never notice them."

"How would you bear the estrangement of those who should naturally be our friends?"

"I shall have your love."

"Disinheritance?"

"Nothing—though, of course, that is impossible, and in time your uncle *will* be appeased."

"No, he will never be appeased. Does disinheritance frighten you?"

"Frighten me! No; but why speak of what can never happen?"

"But it can happen."

"How?"

"My uncle *will* disinherit me."

"He cannot, can he?"

"He can."

"Why, I thought the property was entailed?"

"Not exactly; at all events, my uncle has the power to set the entail aside in a case like this, and he will do so."

"He will?"

"Certainly."

Eila sat quite silent for a minute, with an altered face—a face that changed every instant, showing that all sorts of contradictory thoughts were struggling in her mind. Bertrand looked eagerly at her. At last, as though she had come to a decision, she resolutely disengaged herself from the arm which clasped her, and, standing up in front of her lover, exclaimed, "Then, Bertrand, this engagement must close. I shall break my heart. I shall die soon—the sooner the better; but never, never, never will I be the means of robbing you of your birthright. Oh, why was I ever born? why did I ever see you? wretched, wretched, miserable that I am!" and she sank down in a flood of tears.

"Eila, my own, compose yourself—do try to be calm. I wish I could spare you this pain. It is torture to me to inflict it; but how can you suppose that my birthright is anything to me, compared with you?"

"You shall *never* make this sacrifice for *me*," she replied, vehemently, through her tears and sobs. "I am unworthy of it—I am unworthy of you. You would tire of me, because I am unworthy of you. Your love would wear out, because I am unworthy of it. My beauty, such as it is, would fade, and you would come to hate me. The great opportunities of life would present themselves, and I—I—always I—would be the drag and the barrier—always before you to remind you of your folly. 'For this woman,' you would say, 'I have wasted my life.' No, Bertrand, this can never be. My love, at least, is not selfish. I will not destroy the idol I worship. I would sooner die."

"This is madness, Eila; you must have a small opinion of my love if you can talk seriously in this way."

"It is not so, Bertrand; it is because *my* love is so deep and true that I *can* talk so, and that I will not lay on your love a burden so grievous to be borne. No, you must write to your uncle and say that you bow to his orders —that all—all—is—over between us. Then you must go away, Bertrand, and live in the great world; there you will find plenty of happiness in time, and I—I—I will—oh, let me die! let me die!" she concluded, giving way to a burst of passionate grief.

Bertrand stood up before her.

"You shall not die, sweet love!" he exclaimed; "you shall live to have my love, and give me yours. Nothing that you can do or say can alter my destiny. Cast in your lot with me, then, and fear no change in me. We shall fight the battle of life together. Eila, I am disinherited already."

"I do not understand you."

"The matter stands thus: my uncle's letter made disinheritance the alternative of obedience to his orders. The instant I received it, I wrote and despatched an answer; in it I accepted disinheritance. I abjured my relationship to him. I told him that *I* considered the loss of that connection an advantage rather than the reverse; and, in any case, that, with my feelings for you, my decision would at all times have been the same. I sent this off before I even communicated with you. I did so with a design. I was cunning. I knew your generous nature. I said to myself, 'The noble girl may refuse to let me take this step,' therefore I put the matter beyond a doubt. So don't be cast down, dearest; I am thoroughly and completely disinherited, and by no action of yours."

He spoke triumphantly, as if he was announcing the greatest piece of luck in the world; but the assurance, somehow, did not seem to convey to Eila the expected amount of consolation.

"You should have told me this before, Bertrand," she said, gravely.

"I said it as soon as I could; the fact is, I hardly knew what I was saying; but I am not sorry that I did not tell you at first exactly how matters stood, for it has given me the opportunity of seeing how well I knew you—of proving to myself what a clever fellow I am —how well I foresaw what you would do, and how wise my precautions were," said Bertrand, with a cheery laugh of triumph over his own diplomatic finesse.

"Oh, you must *not* talk of it in that way. It is dreadful—it is all dreadful. Bertrand, I cannot sacrifice you. No, no, it cannot—it can never be. Papa would never sanction it even if I consented, and I cannot disobey papa. I will write myself—I will write to your uncle; I will beg and implore him to forgive you. I will promise never to see you again, if he will only forgive you. I will accuse myself—I will say it was all my fault—even that I entrapped you—that you don't really care for me—that you are anxious for an opportunity of escape, and that I will give it—if he will only, only forgive you."

"Eila, you kill me with these words; this is mere madness—it is generosity run mad. As to my uncle——"

"O Bertrand! stop," cried Eila, with a sudden start, and placing her hand on her heart; "say no more, but take me home. I am ill—I am faint; quick—take me home; this agitation is more than I can bear. My heart! my heart!" and she sank on the bench, apparently in a dead faint.

Poor Bertrand wrung his hands in an agony of grief and fear; he knelt down beside her, and called upon her with passionate cries of love to come back to consciousness—a method of restoration not unfrequently resorted to on such occasions, and with more success than (regarded physiologically) it would appear to merit. On this occasion it was successful: Eila very speedily came back to life with a convulsive shudder, and immediately renewed her prayer to be taken home, and beseeched Bertrand to refrain from all converse on the way. Full of anxiety and alarm, her lover obeyed; and when they arrived at the hotel, she said—

"Now leave me, Bertrand; you must not see me again to-day; I must lie down, and try to get calm. Another scene like this dreadful, dreadful one, would kill me."

"I will run for a doctor."

"No, no; that would frighten every one. No, I must have rest and quiet—these are the only remedies. You had better not go in and see the others. I would rather you said nothing at present of what has passed to them. Good-bye."

"O my darling! my precious darling! when I see you in this state—when I see you so ill, all other troubles seem nothing in comparison."

"You must not be silly, Bertrand; it is nothing serious; I shall be quite well soon."

"I shall walk about all night under your windows, and count the hours till I see you again."

"You must do nothing so foolish. Go away and amuse yourself."

"Amuse myself!"

"Yes; good-bye; I *must* go in."

And she went, and left her lover; and woful was the plight she left him in.

END OF THE SECOND VOLUME.

PRINTED BY WILLIAM BLACKWOOD AND SONS, EDINBURGH.

www.ingramcontent.com/pod-product-compliance
Lightning Source LLC
Chambersburg PA
CBHW030747250426
43672CB00028B/1256